CAMBRIDGE LIBRARY COLLECTION

Books of enduring scholarly value

History

The books reissued in this series include accounts of historical events and movements by eye-witnesses and contemporaries, as well as landmark studies that assembled significant source materials or developed new historiographical methods. The series includes work in social, political and military history on a wide range of periods and regions, giving modern scholars ready access to influential publications of the past.

The Land and its People

Rowland Prothero, Baron Ernle (1851–1937) was an author, land agent and politician, whose public career was particularly concerned with agricultural matters. During the First World War he served as President of the Board of Agriculture, organising a significant increase in agricultural production by bringing more land into cultivation and mobilising the labour of the Women's Land Army and prisoners of war. As food shipping from overseas was increasingly interrupted by enemy submarines, this was vital to the national food supply, and many of his reforms were reinstated in 1939-45. *The Land and its People* was published in 1925, and examines the rural economy at a time of great change. He outlines the social and economic history of agriculture in the nineteenth century, before discussing the recent wartime policies, and how state control of agriculture and the application of scientific methods were changing British farming.

T0381874

Cambridge University Press has long been a pioneer in the reissuing of out-of-print titles from its own backlist, producing digital reprints of books that are still sought after by scholars and students but could not be reprinted economically using traditional technology. The Cambridge Library Collection extends this activity to a wider range of books which are still of importance to researchers and professionals, either for the source material they contain, or as landmarks in the history of their academic discipline.

Drawing from the world-renowned collections in the Cambridge University Library, and guided by the advice of experts in each subject area, Cambridge University Press is using state-of-the-art scanning machines in its own Printing House to capture the content of each book selected for inclusion. The files are processed to give a consistently clear, crisp image, and the books finished to the high quality standard for which the Press is recognised around the world. The latest print-on-demand technology ensures that the books will remain available indefinitely, and that orders for single or multiple copies can quickly be supplied.

The Cambridge Library Collection will bring back to life books of enduring scholarly value (including out-of-copyright works originally issued by other publishers) across a wide range of disciplines in the humanities and social sciences and in science and technology.

The Land
and its People

Chapters in Rural Life and History

Rowland Edmund Prothero

CAMBRIDGE UNIVERSITY PRESS

Cambridge, New York, Melbourne, Madrid, Cape Town, Singapore,
São Paolo, Delhi, Dubai, Tokyo, Mexico City

Published in the United States of America by Cambridge University Press, New York

www.cambridge.org
Information on this title: www.cambridge.org/9781108025300

© in this compilation Cambridge University Press 2010

This edition first published 1925
This digitally printed version 2010

ISBN 978-1-108-02530-0 Paperback

THE LAND AND ITS PEOPLE:
CHAPTERS IN RURAL LIFE AND HISTORY

The Land and its People;

Chapters in Rural Life and History.

By the Right Honble. Lord Ernle, M.V.O.
Formerly Fellow of All Souls College and Honorary
Fellow of Balliol College, Oxford ; late President
of the Board of Agriculture, 1916-19   ::   ::

LONDON : HUTCHINSON & CO.,
PATERNOSTER ROW, E.C.

PREFACE

THE following pages bear, more or less directly, on questions of the moment which are daily assuming graver importance.

The first five chapters deal with a striking change in our social and economic history. It is the transformation of rural districts in the course of the transition from collective to individual farming, the altered position of cultivators of the soil, and the consequent torpor which has fallen on the life of country villages. The interest of the subject is not merely antiquarian : it is living and actual. Nearly every stage in the history is the subject of political, social or economic controversy, though, as it seems to me, the underlying agricultural causes, which influenced and sometimes controlled the movement, have been neglected both by its assailants and its defenders. On the break-up of village farms, one group of politicians found an attack on private property in land. On their revival on modern lines, another group base their hopes of the prosperity of a reorganized agriculture. In the study of their working may lie the partial solution of the problem of labour on the land. For centuries, the English peasantry not only cultivated but occupied the soil. The wage-earning workers of to-day have not forgotten the ideals and traditions of their ancestors, which the unchanging conditions of their industry preserve freshly in their memories. Finally, it may be hoped that a brief sketch of the medieval system may help some dwellers in the country to realize with greater vividness new meanings and interests in their familiar surroundings.

PREFACE

Chapters VI. and VII. deal with the war period of State Control. The Food Campaign of 1916-18 is already ancient history. But it has left its mark on political thought of the present as well as of the future. For a little more than two years, the Government assumed direction of the industry, and created an elaborate organization to make its control and assistance as effective as possible. The partial success which was attained in stimulating production, combined as it was with a period of high wages and standardized prices, has undoubtedly fostered the growth of State Socialism. It is also noticeable that, in the programme of their Land Policy, the Independent Labour Party has accepted in detail the organization created by the Government in 1916-18. A policy adopted to meet war emergencies is not necessarily a safe precedent for peace conditions. For these and other reasons, a record of the Food Campaign, written by the responsible Minister, may be useful.

Chapter VIII. discusses some of the popular charges often made against agricultural landowners, and often based on misunderstanding of facts.

Chapter IX., written in November 1922, lays stress on the difficulty of framing an agricultural policy which will reconcile the divergent interests of farmers in their business with those of taxpayers and consumers. Modern agriculture has been reconstructed on the principle of giving free play to individual enterprise. State assistance in the form of bounties or subsidies could only be given, under our present fiscal system, on terms which would restrict the independence and freedom of farmers. It is wise to explore every possible form of more indirect help which can be given by Governments. But it seemed, and still seems, to me that, until, under the pressure of unemployment, urban wage-earners demand the safeguarding of home industries, farmers must, in the main, meet their

PREFACE

difficulties out of their own resources and by the application of business methods.

Chapter X. is the prophecy of an optimist. No dates are given for the fulfilment of the forecast. It may, therefore, be difficult to disprove the prediction that the future of British farming, except in certain favoured districts, lies in the increased production of bread, meat and milk from land under the plough.

Most of the chapters have been largely rewritten. But their substance has already appeared in the *Quarterly Review*, the *Nineteenth Century*, the *Journals* of the Ministry of Agriculture and of the Royal Agricultural Society, or James Hunter's *Seed Catalogue* for 1923. My thanks are due to the Editors for their permission to reprint such portions as have already appeared.

In conclusion, I desire to thank Mr. Arthur Harrison for the help without which I could not have prepared these pages for the Press.

ERNLE.

CONTENTS

THE LAND AND ITS PEOPLE

CHAPTER I

THE VILLAGE FARM

THE village farm is the core of the agricultural history of England. As compared with its ancient origin, the threefold division of the agricultural interests into landlord, tenant-farmer and wage-earning labourer, as well as the individual occupation and cultivation of agricultural land, are in many parts of this country mushroom-growths. The change from the one to the other has been a slow but continuous process. Already in progress at least as early as the reign of Henry III., it was not completed until the first half of the nineteenth century. Even then the older system has lingered on in remote country districts. Many of us have seen it in active operation. Though now it has been completely superseded, it has left traces which, to the eyes of all who have studied the subject, are deeply impressed, except perhaps in Kent, Devonshire and Cornwall, on the general aspect of England —on the laying out of roads, on place and field names, and on the formation of country villages.

The substitution of the individual occupation and use of agricultural land for the older system of common cultivation was carried out by enclosures. In its effects on the rural population the enclosing movement is an important, and, in some aspects, regrettable development in the social, if not in the economic, history of the country. Its character, causes and conditions have within the last quarter of a century attracted the increasing attention of historical students. Of recent years it has become, for obvious reasons, a favourite battleground of political theorists. For the most part the movement has been exclusively studied in its social and political effects. Emphasis has been rightly laid on the distress caused by the break-up of the agrarian partnerships and on the disastrous consequences of the divorce of the peasantry from the soil. Use has been freely made of a considerable literature of protest and denunciation. The vigorous, picturesque language of sermons, pamphlets and popular verse has been liberally quoted without much discrimination. But very little attention has been paid to the practical questions involved. There is, in fact, a side of the movement which has been unduly ignored by both historians and politicians. It is the agricultural side. So universal has been the reconstruction of the industry on the lines with which we are now familiar, and so completely has the older system disappeared from our midst, that it is necessary to begin with a brief description of the open or common field farms which, two hundred and fifty years ago, still formed half the cultivated area.

The picture must necessarily be a general one. Space allows of nothing else. Wide modifications in the system, due to customary variations or local peculiarities, are so numerous, that in its broad features only is the description universally true. Any examination of the origin of the system would be out of place. To discuss it would be to plunge into the mists of antiquity, and enter on a region of acute controversy, legal, historical, political and social.

The land of a manor in the fourteenth century was divided into three unequal areas. The smallest portion was a compact enclosed block, reserved for the private use of the Lord of the Manor, and held in individual occupation. A far larger part was occupied and cultivated on co-operative principles by the villagers in common, as an association of co-partners, both free and unfree, under a rigid regulated system of management which was binding on all the members of the association. The third part was the common pasture, fringed by the waste in its natural wildness. Over this pasture and waste, common rights were exercised by the Lord of the Manor in virtue of his ownership, by the village partners in virtue of their arable holdings, and by the occupiers of certain cottages to which rights were attached. An inquiry into the farming of the lord's demesne land is outside the scope of the present subject. Originally, the land had been thrown into the village farm. Its gradual withdrawal from the area of common cultivation was the first breach in the system ; but by the middle of the fourteenth century the enclosure of a compact block in individual occupation for the private use of the lord had become very general.

Whether the land was left in the village farm, or enclosed for private use, it was mainly cultivated by the labour services of the open-field farmers, who paid rent in the form of labour on the demesne for their holdings in the village partnership. The legal and social position of these tenant labourers largely depended on the nature of the services which they

thus rendered to their lord.   The highest in the
social scale were those who gave team service;
the lowest were the manual workers, and the more
certain and determinate their labour, the greater
their degree of freedom. Of the demesne land
nothing further need be said, except that the frequent recurrence of such farm-names as Court Farm,
Hall Farm, Manor Farm, or Grange Farm, illustrates
at once the antiquity and prevalence of such a
division of the land.

Isolated farmhouses and buildings were so rare
that they may be said not to have existed, except
on the demesne. Above the tufts of trees which
marked the sites of settlements rose the church, the
mill, and, at a little distance, the manor house.
Gathered in an irregular street were the homes of
the villagers who occupied and cultivated the land
of the open-field farm. Nearest to the village, if
possible along the banks of a stream, lay the meadows. Beyond, stretched the open, hedgeless, unenclosed expanse of arable land. Beyond this,
again, ran the common pastures with their fringe
of fern or heather, or gorse-clad, bushgrown waste.
No part of this area—meadow, ploughland, pasture
or waste—was held in individual occupation ; all
was used in common under regulations as to management by which the whole village community were
strictly bound.

The meadowland was annually cut up into lots,
and put up for hay. From St. Gregory's Day to
Midsummer Day the lots were in this way fenced
off for the separate use of individuals. After the
hay had been mown and carried, the fences were
removed, and the grass became the common pas-
turage of the live stock of the community until the
middle of the following March, when the same process

4

was renewed. Sometimes the meadow lots were attached to the arable holdings, so that the same occupier received the same allotment of grass every year. But the more frequent practice seems to have been to distribute them by an annual ballot among the occupiers of the arable land.

Beyond the meadows lay the arable land of the village, divided generally into three great fields. Each of the three fields was subdivided into a number of flats or furlongs, separated from each other by unploughed bushgrown balks of varying widths. These flats were in turn cut up into a number of parallel acre, half-acre, or quarter-acre strips, divided from one another by similar, but narrower, balks, and coinciding with the arrangement of a ploughed field into ridges and furrows.

Year after year, in unvarying succession, the three fields were cropped in a compulsory rotation. One field was under wheat or rye ; the second under barley, oats, beans and peas ; the third lay fallow. It is scarcely necessary to add that roots, temporary grasses, and potatoes were unknown to the Middle Ages, and did not come into general use on farms until the latter half of the eighteenth century. Each partner in the village farm held a bundle of strips in each of the three fields. Thus, if his arable holding was thirty acres, he would every year have ten acres under wheat or rye, ten acres under the other corn crops, and ten acres fallow. No attempt could be made to improve the quality of the soil and bring it up to a general average. Equality could only be secured by distributing the different qualities evenly among the partners. In order to divide the good, moderate and poor land fairly, the strips which the partner held in each field were widely scattered so that no two were contiguous.

The Village Farm

From seed-time to harvest the strips were held in separate occupation for the private use of the individual holder. After harvest, and until the next season's cultivation, the live stock of the community wandered over the fields under the care of the common herdsman, shepherd and swineherd.

There were, therefore, common grazing rights at certain seasons of the year over the whole of the meadow and arable land of the partnership. There was also the common pasture of the manor and village farms which lay beyond the meadows and the arable fields. It was fringed by the border of waste which provided fern or heather for litter and thatching, hurdle-wood, and tree-loppings for winter browsing, furze and turves for fuel, acorns and mast for swine, as well as large timber for fencing implements or building. For the enjoyment of these lesser common rights to the produce of the waste, small annual payments were usually made by the village farmers to the manorial lord. Still more important were the common pastures. When the aftermath of the meadows was gone, and the fallows and stubbles were ploughed, they supplied the only keep for the live stock, which, at the best, barely survived the winter as skin and bone. They were therefore highly prized and jealously guarded by the partners in the village farm as an essential and integral part of their holdings. The modern and popular idea of a common is inapplicable to medieval commons. The general public had no share in or claim to their use. On the contrary, they were rigidly excluded ; the live stock of strangers were driven off ; cottages built upon them were pulled down ; commoners who turned out more cattle than they were entitled to were " presented " and fined. Those who enjoyed the common rights over pasture and waste were known and definite individuals. They were, as has been said, the manorial lord in virtue of his ownership, the partners in the village farm, who in theory, were limited in the number of stock which they could turn out, by the size of their arable holdings, and the occupiers of certain cottages to which the rights were attached. To them the pastures were common, and to no one else. The rest of the world were trespassers.

Some of the partners in the village farm were freemen, some were serfs; between the two ends of the scale were men who socially, if not legally, held intermediate positions. Their arable holdings were of different sizes, and were held by a great variety of titles and tenures. A few of the occupiers of land or cottages were freeholders; the great majority were tenants, holding their title from the landowner by widely diversified tenures. Some were copyholders for lives and, later, of inheritance; others were leaseholders for lives or for terms of years; others were tenants from year to year or at will. Equally varied were their rents. Some were held by military service; others by team labour on the lord's demesne; others by manual labour, more or less fixed or uncertain; others paid fixed money rents; others produce rents; others a combination of the two. But the great point was that practically the whole of the inhabitants of the village, as freeholders, or tenants, or squatters who had made good their title to encroachments by length of occupation, had some interest in the soil other than that of wages. Few, if any, were landless wage-earners. Even the serfs had some stake in the community, though in the eye of the law they were propertyless.

The open-field farm was, in many ways, well

suited to the times in which it flourished. In the early Middle Ages, each agricultural community, with its graduated degrees of dependence and its collective responsibility, was organized, like a trade guild, for mutual help and protection. The organization supplemented the weakness of the law, which was often powerless to safeguard the rights of individuals ; the manorial courts, for many years, to some extent supplied the place of assizes, quarter sessions, and county courts. Socially and agriculturally, the system was also adapted to a disturbed and unsettled period. Communities grouped in villages were safer from attack than if the individuals were isolated in detached farm-houses. Their co-operative principle enabled them to maintain, in spite of the frequent absences of able-bodied men on military service, some degree of continuity of cultivation. Their rigid rules of management may have hindered improvement ; but they certainly, as long as the soil remained productive, checked wholesale deterioration. Economically they had not yet become detrimental to the national interest. Towns were few and sparsely inhabited. Except in their immediate neighbourhood, there was little or no demand for agricultural produce beyond the needs of the producers themselves. If the land fed those who farmed it, it might be said to have done its national duty. No distant markets needed supplies of food. Each village community was self-supporting and self-sufficing. Nothing was expected of the soil except that it should meet the want of the necessaries of life in the locality where it was situated. The inhabitants held little intercourse with their neighbours. Except along the main thoroughfares they had few means of communication. Such local roads as existed were mere drift ways, often impassable in the winter except on foot or on horseback. Little was either sold or bought. Every group of village farmers grew its own bread supply ; its land or its live stock provided its wants of meat, drink, fuel or clothing.

Agriculture, still in its comparative infancy, was unprogressive. No improved methods or increased resources were offered to farmers, which could only be introduced on open-fields with the unanimous consent of a timid and ignorant body of partners, any one of whom could refuse to have them adopted on the farm. The system fostered stagnation, and starved enterprise ; but so long as population and farming remained stationary, no definite economic loss counterbalanced its many social advantages. Obviously, however, occasions might arise when the economic loss might be so great as to outweigh the social gain. When such occasions arose, the reconciliation of the two divergent claims presented a very difficult and complex problem. It cannot honestly be said that the wisdom of our legislators found any satisfactory solution. The variety of interests involved, and of rights enjoyed, some capable of legal proof, others originating in encroachments, others existing only by sufferance, required, if they were to be fairly adjusted, most careful discrimination. They sometimes received scant attention, and, under the pressure of economic necessity, the social advantages were unduly sacrificed.

Even in the infancy of farming the agricultural defects inherent in the common cultivation of land by the open-field system are many and obvious. As farming skill advanced, the objections to it became more and more serious. At first, and so long as the virgin soil retained its natural fertility, these defects were mitigated. But their existence was very early recognized by practical men. The waste of arable land was considerable, owing to the innumerable balks and footpaths. Still more serious was the waste of time and labour. The buildings were sometimes as much as two miles from the holdings. A holder spent hours in visiting his scattered strips, and the toil of minor tillage operations was enormously increased by the distances between the different parts of his arable land. The distinction between grass and arable was permanent, though both might profit by conversion.

All the occupiers were bound by rigid customary rules, compelled to treat all kinds of soil alike, unable to differentiate in their cultivation, bound to the unvarying triennial succession, obliged to keep exact time with one another in sowing and reaping their crops. Each man was at the mercy of his neighbours. The idleness of one might destroy the industry of twenty. If one partner cleaned his strip, his labours might be wasted by the foul condition of the next. Drainage was practically impossible. If one man water-furrowed his land, or scoured his courses, his outfalls might be choked by the apathy or slovenliness of his neighbour. The supply of manure was inadequate. It need scarcely be said that there were no artificials. Natural fertilizers only existed. The value of town refuse, and other substances, were known to the Middle Ages. So also were the uses of marl and lime and chalk. But such fertilizers, if procurable, were often too costly for small open-field farmers. The dung of their live stock was generally their only resource, and it was wasted over the wide expanse of pasture which the cattle traversed in pursuit of food. Unable to supply adequate winter keep, and possessing few separate closes, open-field farmers reared calves and lambs under every disadvantage. Ill-fed all the year round, and half starved in the winter, the live stock dwindled in size. The crowding of the sheep and cattle on the over-stocked and practically unstinted pasture, or in the common-fold on the stubbles, favoured the generation of all kinds of disease. Stock-breeding on improved lines was an impossibility.

The remedy for many of these defects was individual occupation. A freeholder whose land lay in an open-field farm was only half an owner ; a leaseholder found the value of his lease similarly reduced. Only on enclosed land, separately occupied, could men secure the full fruit of their enterprise. To some extent the effective and practical working of the system was increased without substantial change in its framework. It very early became a practice to take in closes for various purposes, especially for working oxen or other live stock ; or to make temporary or permanent enclosures from the pasture common, which were often brought under the plough and formed the " ancient inclosures " of eighteenth century awards ; or even to enclose portions of the common arable land, a practice known as " several in open." These were useful adaptations of the ordinary common-field system. But they scarcely touched the fringe of the most serious difficulty.

The worst feature in the existing system was the inevitable and progressive decline in the productivity of the soil. Land can be continuously cropped for corn, if it is kept clean, well-drained and adequately manured. But the arable land of open-fields was often foul. The balks harboured twitch ; the fallows left their triennial heritage of docks and

The Village Farm

thistles. The heavy seeding required for crops points to the necessity of preventing the corn from being smothered by weeds. Drainage, with the appliances which medieval farmers commanded, was always a puzzle, and on the open-fields the task was made harder by the difficulty of obtaining agreement among the contiguous occupiers of the intermixed strips. The supply of manure was always inadequate, and what there was did not always go on the land. It is known from writers of the seventeenth and eighteenth centuries that straw and dung were often mixed into balls and used for fuel. Triennial fallows were no sufficient substitutes for clean farming, drainage and fertilizers. Much was taken from the soil and little replaced.

Strong evidence exists to show that, in the fourteenth and fifteenth centuries the arable land, continuously cropped for corn for several hundred years, was losing its fertility. The yield was falling. Land which had produced a livelihood for a man and his family, ceased to supply his necessary food. Portions were being abandoned as tillage. There was difficulty in finding tenants before, as well as after, the Black Death. Fines were paid for the privilege of refusing an inheritance in a holding. Tenants were often obtainable only under compulsion. The obvious remedy was to give the arable land a prolonged rest under grass, and to bring the pastures under the plough in substitution. How to effect this necessary change was one of the agricultural problems of our ancestors. So far as the demesne land of the manorial lord was concerned, it could be withdrawn from the open-field farm and separately cultivated. When Fitzherbert wrote in 1523 that process was, as to portions of the owner's land, practically complete. Some relief was obtained by bringing under the plough new land reclaimed from the forests. In some cases, portions of the common pasture were ploughed. In others, the partners in the open-field farms were encouraged to agree to exchange and consolidate their holdings, or to take in separate closes out of the arable fields. Thus pasture made its way into the area hitherto devoted to the plough. None of these remedies, though each entailed enclosure, broke up the framework of the agrarian partnerships. They were rather devices to adapt the old system to changing needs, and were extensively practised in the fourteenth and fifteenth centuries. With their extension began to grow up a new class of landless labourers for hire.

Enclosures of these types aroused no storm of criticism. But they did not meet the real difficulty. That difficulty was, as has been said, the falling productivity of the arable land. With this decline the majority of the partners in open-fields were, individually and collectively, too poor to grapple. The more substantial men might have met it by agreeing to such a rearrangement of the arable and pasture land as would enable them to lay down the ploughland to grass, and bring the grass under the plough. But their poorer neighbours could not have borne the cost of the readjustment. The decline, therefore, continued, and was accentuated by the effects of social and political changes. The feudal system was breaking up, and labour services were being exchanged for money rents. So feeble was the demand for land that the occupiers were able to drive hard bargains. Substantial men profited by the change ; but it was otherwise with those who were less well off. The poorest tenant might pay his rent by work on the lord's lands ;

but if he had to pay in money, he might have to sacrifice stock, and so set his foot on the slippery slope which leads to destitution.

The long French wars of the fourteenth and fifteenth centuries, followed by the Wars of the Roses, were not a period when agriculture was likely to thrive. There is direct evidence that farming was actually deteriorating in its methods. Fitzherbert notices that several useful farming practices had fallen into disuse. One is that of marling or liming, the value of which was well known to medieval farmers at a very early period. His comparative silence on the subject of drainage indirectly points towards the same deterioration. Neither he nor Tusser mention the shallow drains, filled with stones and turfed over, which were familiar to the farmers of the fourteenth century. To the impoverished occupiers the cost of draining or manuring had become prohibitive, and perhaps, in these and other details of management, the relaxation of the minute supervision of manorial officials was telling its tale. Even without this deterioration in farming practices, the loss of fertility was becoming sufficiently serious. If soil exhaustion continued unchecked, it threatened to become fatal to many of the open-field farms. The weaker men would go to the wall. The men of substance would meet the decline by exchanging their intermixed strips, and consolidating their holdings. This change was in progress. But with the agricultural resources then available, the most efficient remedy was the conversion, on a large scale, of arable into pasture, and of pasture into arable. It was only with the greatest difficulty that this change could be effected without destroying the framework of the old agrarian partnerships.

Extension of Pasture

At the end of the fifteenth century, the enclosing movement, which had been in progress for many years in a piecemeal form, began to proceed on a more comprehensive scale. It assumed a new shape which was subversive of the village farm and led to depopulation, because it enclosed the open-fields and converted them to pasture. Instead of bringing the common pasture under the plough in substitution for the older arable land, it laid down the whole area to grass. Its effect on the rural population seized on the popular imagination. A considerable literature of protest and denunciation sprang into existence. Commissions were appointed to inquire into and report on the movement ; numerous Acts of Parliament were passed to prevent or regulate its progress. The period 1485–1560 is the first of the two great periods of enclosure which form the special subjects of the following chapter. The second is roughly covered by the reign of George III., 1760–1820.

Both in the sixteenth and in the eighteenth century, writers neglected the agricultural side of the movement. Public attention was fastened on its social effects. Popular passion was excited by the preachers, pamphleteers and ballad writers, who denounced, in the racy language of Tudor times, the " greedy gulls," " idle cormorants " and " caterpillars of the commonwealth " who eat up the patrimony of the poor. The same appeals were repeated in the eighteenth century—and since. To a certain extent they were well-founded. Both periods were epochs of great industrial changes, and in both, the rural population suffered. To some extent the complaints were and are justified. No concerted effort was made to secure, by every means compatible with the national interest, the hold of

The Village Farm

the rural population on the land. But at both the Tudor and the Hanoverian periods, it is fair to remember that the industrial prosperity of the nation was involved in the enclosing movement. In the first it was the growth of the woollen trade ; in the second it was the development of manufacture. In both the peasant was sacrificed. Nor can the agricultural motive of the change be ignored. Under the Tudors the progressive infertility of the arable land stimulated enclosure : under George III. the turnip and artificial grasses lent powerful aid to an agricultural revolution. From this point of view the variation in the ground of resistance is significant. The Tudors feared that the break-up of village farms would make bread-corn scarce ; the Hanoverians dreaded that, if the village farms were not broken up, they would be starved. The change of attitude is due to the accumulation of new resources of productivity which could only be utilized on enclosed farms.

CHAPTER II

ENCLOSURE OF VILLAGE FARMS

AGRICULTURALLY the main objection to the ancient system of common cultivation was its want of flexibility. Under its rigid rules the methods of farming and the use of land remained for centuries unaltered. But Nature defies human regulations. One great change was in progress, and that was the declining fertility of the open-field farms. A holding of fifteen arable acres—and the majority were probably less—which had in the thirteenth century provided the necessary food for a family, failed to produce it two hundred years later. The virgin richness of the soil was long exhausted ; year after year, much had been taken out and little put back ; considerable tracts of land could no longer be profitably tilled for corn.

Reliable statistics are not available on so extensive a scale as to demonstrate in conclusive fashion the degree to which the yield had declined. But such figures as can safely be used seem to show that, even on demesne lands in the fifteenth century, as compared with the thirteenth, the produce of wheat per acre had fallen. They also suggest that a smaller area was under wheat ; in other words, that only the best soil was tilled for corn, and that inferior land had dropped out of arable cultivation because it no longer produced enough to make tillage profitable. It is not unreasonable to infer that the open-field farms were in no better plight. It is extremely improbable that the lands enclosed for the private use of manorial lords were naturally inferior to those left in common cultivation, and the folding rights of the manor secured the largest and most concentrated supply of manure to the demesne. Where land was in separate occupation, tillage could be converted into pasture and *vice versâ*. Under the rigid system of common cultivation no such change was possible. Once under the plough always under the plough was the rule. Though no figures are recorded to show the yield of open-field farms, it is natural to suppose that the decline in production on village farms was as great, if not greater. To the smaller partners in the associations the failure of fertility meant progressive destitution. They had no means of arresting the decline, which showed itself in the abandonment of portions of ploughland, and the frequent appearance of " leas " in the midst of the arable fields.

Evidence exists to show that, in the fifteenth century, many holders recognized the hopelessness of their prospects by their refusal or reluctance to take land. From natural causes the open-field system was breaking down on the lighter lands. Soil exhaustion was squeezing out the smaller men. A man with fifteen arable acres, yielding ten bushels to the acre, had, deducting seed, a bread supply for five persons from the five acres annually under wheat. If the yield was reduced to five bushels or less, the bread-corn only sufficed for two-and-a-half persons. Much of the poverty and misery of the rural population in both the great periods of enclosures may be fairly attributed to the decreased productivity of the land, though, before the later period, the peasant had been able to supplement the scanty yield of the soil by the money earnings of his domestic industries. When these handicrafts were swept into factories the open-field system, unless it could be so modified as to allow the adoption of new agricultural resources, was doomed to disintegration by its own inherent defects.

It is only just that this central agricultural fact should be borne in mind in approaching either of the two great periods when the continuous process of enclosure excited the strongest criticism. In 1485–1560 the only remedy for the exhaustion of fertility was the conversion of the worn-out arable land into pasture, and the substitution of existing grass-land for the necessary tillage. In 1760–1820 there was an alternative remedy. It lay in the adoption of the newly-discovered resources of the farmer, the introduction of clover, temporary grasses and roots, and the application of the more abundant manure which the increased facilities for stall feeding in the winter months provided. In the earlier period, the first remedy was adopted, in the later period, the second. In both the agency was enclosure, either of a part of the land or on a scale which involved the break-up of the agrarian partnerships. Commercial motives, no doubt, operated to accelerate both changes. There was money to be made by enclosures. But from the economic point of view the movement was justified by the national interest in the maximum yield from the soil of the country.

Within the framework of the open-field system enclosure was at work. The weaker men were dropping out, and the more substantial men were

Enclosure of Village Farms

taking up the vacated holdings. By arrangement among the tenants there was also an interchange and consolidation of intermixed strips. In both cases the change was often followed by piecemeal enclosure for separate use, either temporary or permanent. But the process was so slow that it excited little comment or apprehension, though its social effect was to increase the growing number of landless wage-earners. The smaller holders who were able to survive, did so through the common rights of pasture. If their arable strips yielded little or no produce, their retention carried with them the right to pasture their live stock. Even where a man had vacated his arable holding, he still clung to the privileges which it had conferred, especially the common shackage in the stubbles of the open-fields. Many of the common rights thus exercised were a breach of the open-field system, and had their origin in sufferance or encroachment.

It was not till the period 1485–1560 that the enclosing movement, long in progress, reached a height which alarmed the country. The ephemeral literature to which it gave birth must be taken with the proverbial grain of salt. There was much exaggeration as well as truth in the description of its social consequences. The contemporary explanation, widely disseminated, was that the progress of enclosures, and the extensive conversion of tillage to pasture, were due to the greed of land-owners. Tempted by the high prices of wool, so ran the charge, the landowners, and especially the new ones, evicted the open-field farmers from the arable land, meadows and common pasture of the village farms, and turned the whole into sheep walks. A shepherd and his dog took the place of populous hamlets. Sheep " that were wont to be

Depopulation

so myke and tame, and so smal eaters '' turned into
devourers of human beings :

> They have eate up our medows and our downes,
> Our corne, our wood, whole villages and townes ;
> Yea, they have eate up many wealthy men,
> Besides widowes and orphane children.

The general truth of this picture is confirmed by
the eloquent pen of Sir Thomas More. That
enclosures, where the whole area was laid to grass,
led to depopulation cannot be disputed. In particular instances the popular charge was true. It
may be questioned whether those instances were
typical or exceptional. At this distance of time it
is difficult to give any certain or definite answer.
But the evidence collected by the Commissions of
the sixteenth and seventeenth centuries goes to
show that enclosures of whole townships were rare.
The period coincides with the break-up of feudal
households, the Dissolution of the Monasteries, and
industrial reconstruction. A flood of pauperism
swept over the country, and no doubt agricultural
changes contributed to its volume. Numerous
insurrections attest the discontent of the rural
populations. It suited the dominant political party
to emphasize the agrarian causes and to ignore those
which originated in the vast religious changes that
were taking place.

It may also be worth while to notice the nature
of the motive to which enclosures were attributed.
It was alleged that, owing to the great development
of the woollen manufactures in the early Tudor
period, the price of wool rose to such a height as to
encourage the abandonment of corn-growing for
sheep-runs. No doubt commercial motives of this
nature accelerated enclosures. But if, during the

period when enclosures were proceeding most rapidly, the price of wheat remained relatively higher than that of wool, some additional reason other than trading profit must be found for the conversion of arable into pasture. That reason, it is suggested, is supplied by the exhaustion of the existing corn-land, especially on open-field farms, and by the necessity of restoring its fertility by a prolonged rest under grass. Thus sheep were as much a by-product or result of enclosure as they were its direct object or cause.

This view is confirmed by the trend of prices. Enclosure of a piecemeal kind had been going on throughout the fifteenth century ; it received a great expansion in the forty years following 1485, and took, more and more, the shape of grass and sheep farming. Was the rise in the price of wool, relatively to that of wheat, so great as to afford a sufficient temptation to make the change ? During the whole of the period 1270 to 1430 the price of wool had been consistently higher than that of wheat. But from 1430 to 1540—the period during which the progress of enclosures excited most alarm, and was attributed to the superior profits of sheep-farming—this relation was reversed, and the price of wheat, in every decade but one, was higher than that of wool. It is true that in 1541–50 the price of wool suddenly soared high above that of wheat, but that was after the original force of the movement was to some degree spent. The general trend of prices seems to show that the usual explanation of the immense profits derived from sheep-farming will not satisfactorily account for the extension of pasture.

It is not disputed that the extension of sheep-farming was one of the causes of enclosures in 1485–1560. But it is argued that, in many cases, sheep-

Legislation against Enclosure

walks were themselves the effect of an underlying cause, namely the decline in the productivity of the soil. The only remedy lay in the restoration of the fertility of the exhausted arable land by conversion to pasture. The legislature endeavoured to cope with the situation by a series of Acts of Parliament directed against engrossing and enclosing. Engrossing meant the accumulation of holdings in the hands of one man. The law attempted to check an economic process, which was the inevitable answer to exhausted fertility, by preventing any individual from holding more than one farm. The word "farm," which originally meant the stipulated rent for an area of land, had not yet acquired its present meaning of the area of land out of which the rent issues. It was in the transition stage of meaning the definite area of land which afforded a living to a man and his family. It is in this sense that the word is used by Tudor legislators. They meant the additional occupation by one individual of the ten, fifteen or thirty arable acres which had once afforded a living to another partner in the open-field farm. They did not inquire whether the area would still have afforded a living. They clapped a plaster to the sore, instead of attempting to remedy the sore itself, which was the exhausted fertility.

Tudor legislators in a similar way dealt with enclosing. It was easy to pass an Act of Parliament that the open-field system must be maintained and that the arable land must be retained under the plough. But, if the land did not return a living under tillage, the Act was a dead letter. At the time it was a frequent complaint that the legislation proved ineffective to check the progress of enclosures. One of the principal reasons why so little attention was paid to the law was, that it provided no remedy for the evil it proposed to prevent. It was therefore as powerless as a Pope's Bull against a comet.

It was not until the close of the sixteenth century that this fact was officially recognized. Alderman Box, in 1576, wrote a remarkable memorial to Lord Burleigh, in which he urges the folly of attempting to force men to continue to grow corn on exhausted arable. Twenty years later, the principle found legal sanction. A statute at the end of the reign of Elizabeth (1597) recognizes the difficulty. Men were relieved from the penalties attached to the conversion of tillage to grass, if they laid down arable to pasture with the " intente " that such " Grownde shall recover Harte and Strengthe." The change was welcomed by an agricultural member of the House of Commons in the debate on the Bill. " For it fareth with the earth," he says, " as with other creatures that through continual labour grow faint and feeble-hearted, and therefore if it be so far driven as to be out of breath, we may now by this law resort to a more lusty and proud piece of ground while the first gathers strength. . . . And this did the former lawgivers overslip, tyeing the land once tilled to a perpetual bondage and servitude of being ever tilled." Even in Tudor times, it would seem that Parliament sometimes misunderstood or neglected agricultural difficulties.

It would be interesting to trace the influence of soil on the progress of enclosure. If, for instance, it could be established that the lighter soils were the first to be enclosed, and that, where the soil was deep and rich, or where, on chalk lands, the farmers commanded a ready means of maintaining fertility, the village farm retained its hold, the view that soil exhaustion was one of the principal causes behind the movement would be strikingly confirmed. It is obvious that the loss of fertility would be first felt on the lighter land, and that the richer soils would hold out longest. Much evidence might perhaps be quoted in support of this opinion. But there was so little uniformity in the movement, and it was affected by so many other local considerations, that any generalizations would be unsafe. New industrial districts were opening out as woollen manufactures developed; towns were increasing in size; means of communication were improving. Agriculture could not, in these changing circumstances, long continue in the self-supporting stage to which open-field farms were adapted. It was no longer enough that producers should feed themselves. Surplus produce was needed for the support of industrial districts and urban populations.

On purely agricultural ground the defence of the old system was rapidly breaking down. Fear of depopulation had not been the only motive which had inspired the early legislation against enclosures. Scarcely less important as a motive was dread of a loss of bread supplies by the reduction of land under the plough. The fear was crystallized in the Elizabethan prophecy : " No balks, no corn " —in other words, that no grain would be grown on enclosed land. But alarm on this score soon proved to be a bugbear. The supply was greater than before. The area under corn rather increased than diminished. The average yield of wheat per acre also rose on the new land brought into cultivation, and on the older arable when it was re-converted to tillage, until it is said to have reached twenty bushels. These results were recognized in 1619 in the appointment of a Commission to grant

Enclosure of Village Farms

licences for the conversion of arable land to pasture. After referring to the old legislation on the subject, the Proclamation states that " the quantitie and qualitie of errable and corne lands at this day doth much exceed the quantitie that was at the making of the saide Lawe." It goes on to say that, as the want of corn " shall appeare or the price thereof increase, all or a great part of those lands which were heretofore converted from errable to pasture and have sithence gotten heart, strength and fruitfulness, will be reduced to Corne lands againe, to the greate increase of graine to the Commonwealth and profite to each man in his private." With occasional rises in price, due mainly to bad seasons, civil war, or currency disturbances, the supply of corn for the next hundred and eighty years was abundant, steady and relatively cheap, in spite of the growing population and considerable exports of grain which continued up to the beginning of the long war with France.

With ocular demonstration that corn-growing could and would flourish on enclosed land, the discussion of the open-field system enters on a new phase. Attention begins to be increasingly concentrated on the obstacles which village farms presented to the introduction of improved farming, and on the economic loss that they inflicted on the community by their waste of land. Agriculturally, the interest of the Elizabethan and Stuart periods lies in the numerous improvements in methods and in the increased resources which were suggested to farmers. Between 1577 and 1689, the suggestion of new practices, new crops and new rotations is multiplied. Most of the changes which have revolutionized British farming in the nineteenth century were discussed and foreshadowed in agricultural literature.

It is from this new point of view that open-field farms are discussed. New and formidable arguments are based on the new means of agricultural progress. On the arable land of open-fields, subject to common rights while fallow or from corn-harvest to seed-time, it was impossible to introduce the new crops. Rotations were limited and fixed by immemorial usage. No individual could move hand or foot to effect improvements, without the unanimous agreement of the whole body of joint occupiers. If one man sowed turnips, it would be the live-stock of the community that would profit. Better stock-breeding was impossible when all the grazing was in common. The difficulties of drainage were enormously increased by the necessity of securing co-operation. To these new arguments must be added the agricultural condition of many of the village farms. The evidence on this point may be, to some extent, prejudiced, because it comes from the advocates of progress. But it is so uniform in tenor and character, so confirmed by previous experience, and so consistent with the natural results to be expected from the rigidity of open-field farming, that it must be allowed some weight. The yield of the arable land on village farms was comparatively small and poor in quality. The commons were "pest-houses of disease," and the live-stock that were reared on them were dwarfed and undersized. Large quantities both of the arable and pasture were worn out. Many open-field farmers lived "worse than in Bridewell."

The argument drawn from improved methods and increased resources would have been more

Enclosure of Village Farms

forcible if the suggested changes had been put in practice by the majority of tenants on enclosed land. What was wanted was a lead, and in the eighteenth century it was given by the landowners. They initiated experiments and poured their money into the land. Farms were at great cost adapted to modern methods by new buildings, roads, fences and drainage. Much of the land was literally " made " during the period. A wave of agricultural enthusiasm rose with each decade of the century, until at last it swept over the country. The introduction of roots, clover and artificial grasses solved the problem of winter keep. It enabled farmers to carry a larger head of stock. More stock yielded more manure ; more manure raised larger crops ; larger crops supported larger flocks and herds, which were both better bred and better fed. The agricultural circle seemed to promise indefinite expansion.

The effect of this agricultural revolution on village farms is obvious. The stream of prosperity passed them by. They were, so to speak, medieval back-waters. Unless their system was transformed they could not adopt the improvements which, on enclosed land, were so marvellously increasing production. Yet still, so long as population remained stationary and food was abundant, the old battle was renewed again and again. On one side was pleaded the injury which the break-up of village farms and the partition of commons inflicted on small occupiers and commoners. On the other were urged, with ever-increasing force, the obstacles to farming improvements which were presented by open arable fields, the unprofitable use of land occupied in common, and the commercial and productive advantage of enlarged

separate holdings. Much was still to be said on
both sides. It remained a question of the balance
of national advantages.

In the early part of the century the village
farms dropped out gradually and slowly. Enclosure Acts were now the recognized procedure
in enclosing open-fields, commons and wastes.
From the reign of Anne to the accession of
George III. their number was small, and some of
the earliest included in the list were confirmatory
of previous arrangements. From 1760 onwards,
they rapidly multiplied under the pressure of necessity. England was suddenly becoming a manufacturing country. Population was shifting to the
North, and collecting into towns. From these
new industrial centres more and more loudly came
the demand for food. Little room was left for an
agricultural system which was only self-supporting.
Some effort was made to adapt it to the changing
conditions. An Act of Parliament in 1773 enabled
a majority of partners in the agrarian association
to compel the consent of the minority to adopt
the new crops in their rotations. Here and there,
but with extreme rarity, instances are recorded
of the introduction of turnips or clover in open-
fields. The Act may not have been made known
or pushed with sufficient vigour in rural districts.
Anyhow it proved a failure. Enclosure was no
longer a question only of social or agricultural
advantage ; it had become one of economic necessity. The pressure steadily increased in severity.
It culminated during the Napoleonic War, when
every pound of food became of national value.

At the declaration of peace in 1815, the old
system of common cultivation had practically disappeared, and the newer system of individual

occupation was being universally installed in
its place.   Socially the change was a loss ; economically it was justified.   Under the new agricultural
system Great Britain had been enabled to keep
pace with her expanding needs, and, out of her
own agricultural resources, not only to stand the
strain of twenty-two years of war, but in 1840 to
supply bread and meat to a population which, as
compared with 1760, had more than doubled.   It
was a task which, unless centuries of experience
were reversed, could never have been accomplished
by the ancient system of village farms.

CHAPTER III

OBSTACLES TO PROGRESS

BETWEEN the two great periods of enclosure,—between, that is, the sixteenth century and the second half of the eighteenth century, the case for the enclosure of village farms was immensely strengthened by the accumulation of new resources of farming. Experience had demonstrated that the supply of bread-corn was rather increased than diminished by the consolidation of holdings in the hands of individuals. Discoveries had been made which could not be put in practice on village farms without drastic alterations in their organization. Adopted and tested on individual tenancies, they had proved their value in raising the productivity of the soil and keeping pace with the growing needs of urban populations. Agriculturally, village farms became obstacles to farming progress. Nor did the enthusiastic advocates of the new methods believe that their adoption would depopulate rural districts. They thought, and rightly thought, that arable farming on the improved lines would necessitate a larger demand for agricultural labour.

For the greater part of the period the new discoveries had been only enshrined in the pages of those strange compounds of wisdom and folly

which compose our earlier agricultural literature.
They appealed as little to individual occupiers as
they did to partners in village farms. What was
needed was proof of their efficiency. When that
had been given, farmers were ready and eager to
put them in practice. In the second quarter of the
eighteenth century the new methods were tested
by the enterprise of large landlords like Turnip
Townshend and gentlemen farmers like Jethro
Tull. The farming community were converted.
They became enthusiasts. Thus, from 1760 onwards, village farms were faced by a new and
formidable foe. The national demand for food
was growing rapidly. It could be met by the
adoption of new practices of recognised value which
could not be introduced upon land cultivated on
medieval principles.

The strength of this agricultural argument is
multiplied, if we realize in detail how many of the
methods, which between 1780 and 1870 made
British agriculture famous, were anticipated and
discussed a century and a half before they came
into general use in this country. The struggle
between practice and science was protracted, and
in its course the story of Joseph and his brethren
was daily re-enacted. The elder sons of Jacob were
plain practical men, experienced in the traditional
routine of stock-rearing and corn-growing, wearing
the weather-stained garments of their industry.
It is possible that their younger brother, with his
dainty clothes and indoor airs, had spoken dis-
respectfully of their lives and methods. He was
a theorist. They may have known that he could
not milk a goat. The day came when they saw
their chance. " Behold this dreamer cometh ! "
So they stripped him of his variegated raiment,

Science and Practice

"his gold spectacles, spats and tall hat," and thrust him into a pit. But Joseph lived to save them from starvation and become their leader. Again and again in subsequent times, science has saved practical agriculturists from ruin.

Yet it must be admitted that farmers had good reason to distrust the pseudo-scientific advice of book-farmers. Before the end of the eighteenth century it was often indistinguishable from quackery, often false in its conclusions, often so mixed with folly as to be ridiculous, often based on hasty generalizations, often so extravagant in its promises as to arouse suspicion. To the theories of would-be teachers the practical man opposed his traditional routine of farm management. Its growth had been slow. It had been built up by protracted processes. Here and there some isolated agriculturist had, either by accident or experiment, chanced upon some new process or substance which increased the yield of his crops. Often the discovery would be ignored or forgotten, perhaps to be revived a century later. Sometimes it would be tried and confirmed by neighbours, spread over an ever-extending circle, and gradually incorporated in the general stock-in-trade of farmers. Tested experience of this kind is not easily disturbed. Why the given results follow may be unknown; it is enough that they are produced. Another process will not be adopted merely because it is new. Proof of better results is needed, and printed pages, especially when reading was a rare accomplishment, carry less weight than ocular demonstration. Seeing is believing. Sound sense often lies behind the conservatism of farmers. Mistakes in agriculture are costly, and sure returns are necessary where subsistence is at stake. The path of the industry is strewn with the wreckage of those who have tried to grow rich by short cuts.

When true science began to speak, it had to remove the mass of suspicion engendered by the quacks who professed to speak in her name. Agricultural chemistry dates from the discovery of the composition of air at the close of the eighteenth century. Before that time, the prejudices entertained by agriculturists against the unverified theories of book-farmers were often justified. They rested on a sure instinct. But rural ruts were so deep that they restricted the horizon. Old agricultural writers often recommended practices, now in universal use, a century before they were adopted. Their new-fangled notions might have enriched the great-grandfather instead of the great-grandson.

The history of agricultural literature printed in English begins with the sixteenth century. In 1520 a Dutch bookseller, named John Dorne, carried on his business at Oxford. His trade was especially brisk at the two great annual fairs in May and October. In his day-book for that year he enters his sales. He sold one copy of " Husbandry " at one penny, and three copies of " Medecens voer Hors " at two-pence each. Both books have disappeared. They have been thumbed out of existence.

The true father of the English literature of the farm is John Fitzherbert. He was a Derbyshire man, whose " Boke of Husbondrye " was printed in 1523. He did not presume to write on farming till he had accumulated a practical experience of forty years. In this restraint he set a good example, which has not always been followed. A shrewd hard-headed man, he wrote a sensible book. Even in those days Derbyshire was famous as a horse-

John Fitzherbert

breeding county. Fitzherbert owned " 60 mares
or more." He knew the trade. He had as little
faith in a horse-dealer or a " horse-leche " as in a
" potycarye." " It were harde," he says, " to
truste the best of them." His object in writing
seems mainly to have been to demonstrate the
superiority of an enclosed farm in separate occupation to a village farm cultivated on the prevalent
system of a tenancy in common. The few improvements which he suggests, and the arguments by
which they are enforced, strike us as antiquated.
Both are now everywhere accepted : but it takes
a heavy hammer and many blows to drive a nail
through heart of oak. It was two centuries and
a half before they were recognized in practice.
He insists on the advantages of a farm in individual
occupation, divided by hedges and ditches into
separate enclosures. In the first instance, he admits,
the expenditure would be considerable, but it
would pay any farmer with a twenty years' lease
to make the outlay. He would get his money
back with interest by saving the charges to common
herdsmen and shepherds and the expenses of hurdles
and stakes, by enjoying the longer season on the
grass which the enclosed land allowed, and by
gaining a greater choice of the time for marketing
his calves and lambs. Enclosed land was better
for the stock and better for the corn.

Fitzherbert did not believe in the abandonment
of tillage or the adoption of ranching. He advocates
mixed husbandry. If a farmer is to prosper, stock
and corn must go together. A man, he says, cannot
thrive by corn unless he has live-stock, and he
who tries to keep stock without corn must either
be " a buyer, a borrower, or a beggar." Though
his resources were limited, though winter-keep

35   3*

remained an unsolved problem, and roots and artificial grasses were still unknown, he sees with a prophetic eye the verification of the maxim that " a full bullock-yard and a full fold make a full stack-yard." If his advice had been heeded in the years 1480-1640, England might have escaped some of the misery which was caused by the transformation of common arable farms into sheep-walks, and by the consequent loss of employment, rural depopulation and destruction of houses and farm buildings.

Half a century later than Fitzherbert came Thomas Tusser, whose " Hundredth Good Pointes of Husbandrie " (1557), afterwards expanded into "Five Hundredth Pointes of Good Husbandrie " (1573), was written in doggerel verse. The book was so popular and so frequently republished that his name cannot be omitted. It is a valuable storehouse of information on existing practices, habits and customs. Tusser was a recorder rather than an improver. He makes no new suggestions, and has no theories to expound. He is an eager champion of the superiority of land enclosed for individual occupation over land occupied in common by a number of occupiers. With Tusser begins the long line of agricultural writers, who failed in the business before they turned to literature, and thus strengthened the prejudice against book-farming. He was " a musician, schoolmaster, serving-man, husbandman, grazier, poet—more skilful in all than thriving in his vocation." He " spread his bread with all sorts of butter but none would ever stick thereon," and he is said to have died in the debtors' prison of the Poultry Counter. Probably his best remembered lines are :

> At Christmas play and make good cheer,
> For Christmas comes but once a year.

Pigeons, Rooks and Crows

On one question, which from time to time is still disputed, both these old authors had made up their minds. Neither had any doubt that rooks were greater malefactors than benefactors. They charge them with preferring grain to grubs. Against pigeons, rooks and crows, Fitzherbert proclaims a crusade. Tusser proposes to arm girls with slings and boys with bows and arrows, to drive away the marauders. Tudor England knew nothing of Board Schools.

One of the few suggestions made in these early books is that of green-manuring. Buck-wheat or "Brank" is suggested for the purpose. In Tudor times the expedient had a special value ; but on village farms it could not be adopted. It smothered the weeds, restored the humus, improved the texture of the soil, and provided manure when dung was scarce. Its use was the greater because the "seeds" crop, which serves similar purposes more effectively, was still unknown. Buck-wheat is a quick grower and a good weed-smotherer. It is for these reasons also recommended by Child (1651). It was sown in May and ploughed in in July. But Mortimer (1707) considered it a better practice to feed it to dairy cattle when it was coming into blossom. If allowed to seed and ripen, the grain was largely used for pigs and poultry. Milled for human food, it made a very white flour, which in Stuart times was highly esteemed for pancakes.

Child mentions other crops for green manure. Tares were, he says, so employed in Kent. He also recommends lupins, probably from his knowledge of Latin writers. The Romans were fully aware of their value before a corn crop, though the scientific reason for the richness of their

37

fertilizing qualities was a discovery of the last century. In the connection may be mentioned another form of catch-cropping. William Ellis of Gaddesden, whose writings were famous in the first half of the eighteenth century, attributes the success of Hertfordshire farmers, among other causes, to growing tares on turnip fallows to be grazed in May. Neither mustard nor vetches seem to have been used for catch-crops.

Fitzherbert and Tusser knew no other country than England. Barnabe Googe was both a traveller and a translator. His " Foure Bookes of Hus-bandrie " (1577) are translated from the Latin work of Conrad Heresbach published at Cologne, and a few pages are added of Googe's own observations on agricultural practices. The farming of the Low Countries with which the book deals, was the most advanced in Europe. But, then as well as subsequently, English farmers looked on foreign innovations with suspicion. They had their full share of the national insularity. In this case they lost an opportunity. Googe gives the first hint of the new resources which, two hundred years later, so marvellously enriched English farmers. He recommended not only the use of rape, but that of what he calls " Trefoil or Burgundian grass." " There can be," he says, " no better fodder devised for cattle." He also suggests, as supplying valuable food for live-stock, the field cultivation of turnips. In the Low Countries they were extensively cultivated in the fields. In England, they were only just beginning to struggle into gardens as vegetables for human use to be " boyled and eaten with flesshe."

Whether Googe succeeded in converting any English farmers to the value of roots and grasses,

Clover and Turnips

is unknown. As he gives a list of men whose farming was an object-lesson to their less advanced neighbours, it is possible that some may have tried the suggestion. If there were any converts, they were few. A dry year may have discouraged the experiment of roots. It may have stiffened the resistance of farmers to their introduction, and confirmed their stereotyped answer that the new crops would not grow in England because their ancestors had never grown them. It was not till more than a hundred and sixty years later that the new resources began, on any general scale, to struggle into use in this country.

In clover and turnips new sources of wealth were thus offered to farmers of land in individual occupation. The want of winter-keep, for instance, accounted for the half-starved condition of English live-stock, which only survived the winter as skin and bone. Here was a partial solution of the problem, and a means of carrying a larger and a heavier head of cattle and sheep. The new crops were destined to be the pivots of mixed farming. Throughout the seventeenth century writers kept pegging away at turnips and temporary grasses. Little attention was paid. In the existing system of open-field farming there was no room for either crop. All the partners in the village farms enjoyed grazing rights over the fallows as well as over the other arable fields from corn-harvest to seed-time. Any enterprising man therefore who wished to grow turnips would grow them for the benefit of his neighbours. Up to 1773, it was impossible, without the assent of all the partners, to alter the rotation by which all were bound, or to interpolate either of the new crops. They were, therefore, out of the reach of village farmers. But occupiers of enclosed farms were almost equally backward in their acceptance.

Once again, seventy years after Barnabe Googe, attention was called to the methods of foreigners by an eye-witness. In a clear and concise treatise, Sir Richard Weston described (1645) the field cultivation of artificial grasses and turnips in Brabant and Flanders. At first the book circulated in manuscript, but it was printed in 1649-50 and again in 1651. Arthur Young, with characteristic enthusiasm, calls Weston " a greater benefactor than Newton," because he offered bread and meat to millions. But the times were unfavourable to progress. Traditionally, Oliver Cromwell interested himself in the introduction of the field cultivation of turnips. He is said to have paid a farmer named Howe a hundred pounds a year for being the first man to grow them successfully in Hertfordshire. Their cause, however, was not helped by the mountebank extravagance of writers like Adolphus Speed (1659), who commends them to farmers as the only food for cattle, sheep, swine and poultry, sovereign for conditioning " Hunting dogs," admirable as an ingredient in bread, supplying " exceeding good Oyl " and " excellent Syder," and yielding " two very good crops each year."

Other writers, on more moderate lines, urged the addition of temporary grasses and turnips to the resources of farmers. Andrew Yarranton, by his personal example and influence, succeeded between the years 1653 and 1677, in establishing clover in Worcestershire and the adjoining counties. He was one of the most interesting men of the time. Starting as a linen-draper's apprentice, he found the " Shop too narrow and short " for his mind. He took leave of his master, lived a country life for some years, served as a soldier in the Civil Wars, turned consulting engineer in 1652, and studied various means of bettering the condition of the country. Impressed with the exhaustion of the " rye-lands " by " long tillage," he suggested clover as the remedy. His " Improvement by Clover " (1663) was " so fitted to the country-man's capacity that he fell on Pell-mell " and the new crop " doubled the value of the Land." Elsewhere, it was long before clover emerged " from the fields of gentlemen " into common use. Jethro Tull, writing in the reign of George I., says that, if advised to sow clover, " farmers would certainly reply ' Gentlemen might sow it if they pleased, but they (the farmers) must take care to pay their rents.' " He thought, perhaps with reason, that his example and advice carried less weight because he was himself a gentleman farmer. In 1768 clover was still unknown in many counties.

Equally strenuous was the opposition to turnips. It must, however, be remembered that at first they were sown broadcast. The name of the first man, Michael Houghton, who grew them at Hawstead in Suffolk in 1700, is preserved. " I introduced turnips into the field," wrote Jethro Tull of Berkshire, " in King William's reign ; but the practice did not travel beyond the hedges of my estate till after the Peace of Utrecht " (1713). In 1716 they were still a source of wonder to the neighbours when they were grown in Scotland by the Earl of Rothes. On the other hand, they made their way more rapidly in Norfolk and Essex where they were established before 1684. Daniel Defoe, who began his tour of Great Britain in 1722, says that Norfolk was the county " where the Feeding and Fattening of Cattle, both Sheep as well as black Cattle, with Turnips, was first practised." Hertfordshire may perhaps dispute the claim. Defoe's " Tour " was published in 1738, the year in which died Lord Townshend, whose zealous advocacy of the use of turnips as the pivot of Norfolk farming gained him the nickname of " Turnip " Townshend.

None of the three Tudor agricultural writers who have been so far mentioned, were men of any scientific pretensions, even in the restricted sense in which the words can be used of our Elizabethan ancestors. Fitzherbert wrote his practical experiences. Tusser recorded facts. Googe reported foreign practices. Sir Hugh Plat was, in the alertness of his mental attitude, more akin to the scientific leaders of the nineteenth century. A man of an ingenious and inventive turn, he farmed near St. Albans. Among his suggested improvements was that of drilling, or, as it was then called, " setting " corn (1600). His attention was drawn to the advantages of the practice by accident. " A silly wench " dropped wheat seeds into the holes meant for carrots. He claimed that, by dibbing wheat instead of sowing it broadcast, a man could increase his yield per acre from four quarters to fifteen. Few farmers were likely to believe so extravagant a promise. But Plat was on the track of a great discovery, although he and his immediate successors took the dibbing of beans as their model, and intended the seed to be deposited by hand. Others worked in the same direction. Francis Maxey (1601) described the new manner of setting corn, and invented a machine which punched holes in the ground.

On similar lines Gabriel Plattes championed the new process so eagerly that he gained the nick-

Drilling of Corn and Roots

name of the " Corn-setter." He rivalled Sir Hugh in the extravagance of his promises. Those who followed his system and used his drill (patented 1639) were promised a hundredfold increase in their yield. He died shirtless, and starving for want of bread, in the streets of London. But agricultural writers did not lose sight of the suggestion. Worlidge, for example, whose " Systema Agriculturae " (1669) deserved, on the whole, in spite of many defects, its reputation as a standard authority, came nearer the mark. He invented a drill to make the furrow, sow the seed, and deposit the manure. The machine is figured and described in his book. But he appears never to have made or tested his implement. Professor Bradley of Cambridge, who (1727) constructed the machine from Worlidge's drawing, found that the instrument would not perform any of its three functions.

It remained for Jethro Tull to invent and perfect a practical drill. It was used for the first time on his farm at Crowmarsh, near Wallingford in Berkshire, somewhere between the years 1699 and 1709. On the drilling of corn and roots he based much of his system of clean farming. By drilling wheat and keeping the soil clean and stirred between the rows, he grew it for many years in succession without manure. Applied to turnips the process trebled their value. But, as he mournfully says, though he grew better crops, at less cost, and with greater economy of seed than his neighbours, none followed his example. It was not till drilling of corn and roots had been enthusiastically adopted in Scotland and thence had drifted back over the English borders into the northern counties, that it gained any general hold in this country, years after Tull's death.

Obstacles to Progress

The most interesting of Sir Hugh Plat's observations are those on manures for arable and pasture land. Once again, it must be noted that, in the use of manure, village farmers were practically restricted to the droppings of their flocks and herds. As a body they were not likely to agree to outlay on the whole of their arable land, and the application to the strips of individuals was prevented by the distance which separated the scattered portions of each holding. Sir Hugh's suggestions are contained in the second part of his "Jewell House of Art and Nature" (1594). He is so enamoured of his subject that manure presents itself to his vision as a Goddess with a Cornucopia in her hand. Basing his theories on Bernard Palissy, he argues that perpetual cropping robs the earth of her vegetative salt. Therefore the wise husbandman must continually replace the elements of its fertility. He recommends a valuable list of manurial substances. He urges that existing practices allowed the vegetative salts of dung to evaporate by long exposure to the sun and so waste the richest properties of farmyard manures. He therefore suggests its accumulation in covered pits. He advises the use of marl, with a warning that it should be proportioned to the needs of different sorts of soil. His other manurial substances include lime, street refuse, the subsoil of ponds, and "watrie bottomes," the brine of Cheshire "salt pittes," ashes, the hair of beasts, malt-dust, soap-ashes, putrified pilchards, entrails of animals or fish, and blood offal.

Fifty years later than Plat, several agricultural writers were busy on the subject of manures. Among them was a man of ingenious and inquiring mind, Gabriel Plattes, the "Corn-setter." His

Manures

" Discovery of Infinite Treasure " was the use of the fertilizing qualities of the substances carried off by water. In the soil of streams, in mud of tidal waves, and in all " coloured " water, he finds the " fatness " of the land. He suggests catch-pits to receive the water of the " land-flouds," especially where they come from fertile fields or paved market-towns. He also advises ditches and sluices to admit tides to run in swiftly and pass out slowly. In both cases, the deposit makes a valuable manure which will fertilize the most barren soil. All " coloured " water should be similarly utilized on the land instead of being allowed to run to waste.

Contemporary with Plattes, were Walter Blith (1649) and Child (1651). Both give lists of manurial substances which supplement the suggestions of Plat. Putting their recommendations together, we get a fairly complete list of the fertilizers recommended for use by agricultural writers of the seventeenth century. They include marl, lime and chalk; farmyard manure, which Child says must not be too much exposed to sun and rain; pigeon and poultry dung; swine's dung, which Fitzherbert says was harmful because it bred thistles; ashes, both of wood and " sea-cole " ; soot; malt-dust; " raggs of all sorts " ; " coarse wooll, nippings and tarry pitch-markes " (Blith); horn, or shavings of horn; seaweed " of all sorts, rotted " (Child); salt dross, " much used on " meadows near Nantwich (Child); marrow-bones (Blith); blood and urine (Child); fish and fish-bones.

Child mentions the New England practice of using on the land a fresh-water fish, called the " Ale-wife, because of its great belly," very full of bones.

It was, he says, caught in weirs, and sold in large quantities to farmers. Both writers suggest mud from rivers, and Child adds " owse " from marshy ditches and foreshores. Both especially recommend a soil full of small shells, taken out of the beds of certain rivers. Child, who calls it " snaggreet," says that it was much used in Surrey. Blith, who calls it " snaylecod," says that one load was worth three of horse or cow dung, that it was found in the Thames Valley and near Uxbridge, and that men gained a " gallant living " by bringing it to the surface and selling it on the river bank at from one shilling and twopence to two shillings and fourpence a load.

Child also recommends, as has been already noted, the practice of green manuring, and the use of lupins for the purpose. Child's " Large Letter " on agricultural improvements is full of useful suggestions. But, in the same breath, he suggests that our live-stock and the agricultural wealth of the country should be increased by the introduction of " Black Foxes, Muske-cats, Sables, Martines," and, above all, the elephant as a useful beast of draught and burden, " 15 men usually riding on his backe together." His advice has not been wholly neglected. In the Cheviots to-day there already exists a flourishing skunk farm, and elsewhere a farm for silver-foxes is projected. The elephant alone, though " not exceeding chargeable," remains unhonoured on the farm.

Jethro Tull, it may be noted, objected to dung as a weed-carrier. In the writings of William Ellis we find the manures actually in use on a Hertfordshire farm in 1733-50, by an advanced farmer. Chalk was largely employed, pits being sunk to obtain the substance. Among the new ingredients are rabbits' dung and rape-dust. London refuse was freely bought; quantities of "cony-clippings, horn-shavings, rags, hoofs, hair, ashes, etc.," were bought from "Mr. Atkins of Clerkenwel." To the manures in use in the country were added, fifty years later, boiled or burned bones, sheep-trotters and malt-dust.

Before the advent of agricultural chemistry, and the establishment of the principles of plant nutrition, the science of manuring was neither studied nor understood in theory. Probably no farmer in the sixteenth or seventeenth century could have explained the precise action of the different substances which he applied. But observation of results by individuals had built up an imposing list of suggested manures, some of which had taken their place in the traditional routine of the best farmers. It is interesting to note that, though the theory was unknown, practical experiment had provided the essential elements of fertility—nitrogen, phosphoric acid and potash. All the native resources, except the coprolite deposits, were in fact utilized. It is the method of using these native materials, in their portable form, and in the discovery and use of new or imported ingredients, such as guano, phosphatic rock, the Stassfurt deposits of potash, or basic slag, that the increased command of fertilizing substances mainly consists.

The effect of cattle droppings is so obvious that dung must have been employed as a fertilizer in the infancy of agriculture in every country. Its treatment might be and may be improved. But it was sheer improvidence, or stark necessity which urged farmers to waste their one natural and all-round manure by mixing it with straw, kneading it into lumps, drying it, and burning it as fuel. Standish (1611) notices the practice. It was evidently wide-spread, for Lawrence (1727) speaks of it as prevailing in Yorkshire and Lincolnshire, and considered it important enough to suggest that all leases should contain a restrictive covenant : " Cowdung not to be burnt for fuel." Arthur Young (1770) found the practice in Buckinghamshire and Northamptonshire. " There cannot," he says, " be such an application of manure anywhere but among the Hottentots," a phrase which he often employs in speaking of village farmers.

To the Romans the value of marl, lime and chalk were known, not as direct plant food, but as indirect fertilizing agencies. There is some evidence that the original home of their use was Britain. But, with the invasion of the Saxons, many practices were temporarily forgotten. The use of these substances may have lingered on in farming tradition ; it may have been revived by ecclesiastical agriculturists from the writings of Pliny, Varro, Columella or Palladius ; it may have been discovered afresh from their effect on the land when thrown up in digging ditches or foundations. Marl was certainly used in the thirteenth century in England. But the practice seems to have fallen into disuse. Fitzherbert, who notices its cost,—it is, he says, " exceeding chargeable,"—regrets that it was becoming obsolete, and Gervase Markham, writing at the close of the sixteenth century, infers from the age of the timber growing in marl pits that they had been abandoned for two hundred and sixty or three hundred years.

Barnabe Googe recommends the use of chalk in moderation ; but he adds the popular saying that " grounde enriched with chalke makes a rich

Marl, Lime and Chalk

father and a beggarly sonne." Its use on the
heavy lands of Hertfordshire has been already
noticed. " Mixing earths," such as chalk on heavy
clay and " red clay " on sandy soils, is one of the
practices to which Ellis attributes the agricultural
success of the county. Large quantities of chalk
were also imported into Essex from Kent, whence
it was brought up the estuaries and distributed
to the farms. The county, it may be added, is
said to have owed its high reputation for farming
to the early date at which its village farms had
been enclosed. Gypsum was another of the substances used, especially in Kent and Sussex. Towards the end of the eighteenth century, its value
was more extensively recognized. When Cornish
or Devonshire farmers brought sea-sand from the
coast on their pack-saddles, they probably did
not know the exact nature of its value, or that
it mainly lies in the carbonate of lime contained
in the broken shells of which it largely consists.
But they anticipated the modern market-gardeners
of Penzance in the use of the substance ; they had
experienced, in some way or other, the utility of
its agency.

Other substances more directly contribute to
plant food. That the value of soot was soon discovered is natural enough. Thrown on some waste
place, its useful properties would be observed.
Whether its effect in raising the temperature of the
soil, or lightening its texture, or deterring slugs
and snails, or its direct fertilizing qualities, commended its use to the first observer, is uncertain.
It was employed, for one or other of these reasons,
in the Middle Ages.

More difficult to explain is the discovery of
the nitrogenous value of such substances as

49   4

"cony-clippings," hair, shavings of horn, or woollen rags. Their effect is so slow that it might be imagined that it would escape detection. Yet they appear in the seventeenth-century lists of manures, and, as has been noticed, were bought by Hertfordshire farmers from London salesmen in the first half of the eighteenth century. Seaweed was extensively used in counties where it was accessible, and in South Wales the practice is especially noticed. Another nitrogenous manure available in maritime counties was fish-waste, such as the "putrified pilchards" suggested by Sir Hugh Plat. For more inland counties there were slaughter-house refuse and dried blood. The valuable properties of malt-dust were, as the lists show, early appreciated and more generally available.

Seventeenth-century writers provided farmers with a considerable choice of nitrogenous manures. They were less rich in their suggestions of substances containing either phosphoric acid or potash. Possibly "snaggreet," the shelly deposit which is mentioned by Child and Blith, may have been mainly valuable as a phosphatic manure. Some phosphates would also be contained in Cornish sea-sand. Otherwise bones were the only available substance. Traditionally their value was observed by a Yorkshire master of fox-hounds on the grass surrounding the kennels. At first they seem to have been roughly broken by hand labour on the farms. But by the middle of the eighteenth century it had become a trade to grind bones for agricultural use, and the value of boiling or steaming them was also recognized. Their use, as has been noted, was recommended by Blith in 1653, and similar advice was given by subsequent writers in the seventeenth century.

Improvement of Live-stock

For potash, farmers depended entirely on ashes. Their use is recommended in all the early lists of manurial substances. Some evidence exists to show that an industry was established for their production and supply. Thus William Ellis, the Hertfordshire farmer, speaks of a potash kiln in Buckinghamshire. It is also on record that, in the eighteenth century, Kentish hop-growers organized a system of collecting the wood-ashes of neighbouring cottagers. Essential though potash is, it is especially valuable in its effect on some of the crops which were the latest comers in English agriculture, such as mangolds and potatoes, the latter of which were recommended by John Forster (1664), but not adopted outside Lancashire on any extended scale till the last century. Both crops have owed much of their later development to the discovery of the Strassfurt deposits.

The illustrations given from agricultural writers of the sixteenth and seventeenth centuries, show that many of the triumphs of modern farming had been anticipated. The materials had been already collected for the great agricultural advance which took place in the last forty years of the reign of George III. It may be added that, as early as 1645, the necessity of securing to tenants the value of their unexhausted improvements had been pleaded. Where so much had been anticipated, one omission on the part of the " Rustick Authours " is striking. There is scarcely any suggestion for the improvement of live-stock. On this side of their subject, writers are meagre and inadequate. None of them discuss the subject with any completeness, or with much regard for varieties of breed or for the different purposes for which animals are bred.

Obstacles to Progress

Worlidge's " Systema Agriculturae " (1669), for instance, passed rapidly through five editions. But the subject " of Beasts " is dismissed in three pages, while one hundred and six pages out of the total number of two hundred and seventeen, are devoted to trees, orchards, gardening, bees and silkworms.

The neglect of stock-breeding and stock-rearing was not unnatural, so long as little fresh meat was eaten, and so long as winter-keep was short, and the stock were herded promiscuously on the commons or in the common folds of village farms. But as the first half of the eighteenth century drew to a close, these practical obstacles were to some extent removed. The market for fresh butcher's meat improved. Farms in separate occupation multiplied. Roots and temporary grasses were creeping into the rotations. When once the improvement in stock-breeding began, it spread with the utmost rapidity. Perhaps farmers adopted the principles laid down by Robert Bakewell (b. 1725; d. 1795) with the greater enthusiasm, because they were the first improvements initiated by one of themselves. The movement owed nothing to book-farmers. It met the needs of a growing demand and afforded an outlet for the natural bent of the genius of English agriculturists; but it could make no progress on a village farm.

Drainage was the only other essential to farming progress which still lagged behind. It had been sensibly discussed by Walter Blith in 1649 and 1652. But the Cromwellian Captain and Puritan, who brings Scripture to enforce his argument, commanded none of the modern appliances, and the concerted use of such methods as were available was difficult, if not impossible, on village farms. Otherwise, the inauguration of the movement for improved live-stock completed the necessary preparations for a great agricultural advance.

The history of agricultural literature in the times of the Tudors or the Stuarts is at once an exhortation and a warning to twentieth-century farmers to keep their eyes open. But it must continually be borne in mind that the new sources of wealth, which were revealed by book-farmers and which passed into general practice, were beyond the reach of the partners in village farms, unless their organization had been drastically improved.

CHAPTER IV

AGRICULTURAL WORKERS IN 1800 AND 1925

THE break-up of village farms greatly increased the number of landless workers for hire. For centuries this class had been steadily growing, as more and more land had been consolidated in individual tenancies and fresh areas brought into cultivation in compact holdings. During the reign of George III. (1760-1820), the process had been so accelerated as to approach the pace of agricultural revolution. The village farm became the exception; the comparatively modern threefold division into landlords, tenant farmers and workers for hire, became the rule. New conditions of employment were created; new problems were set for solution.

Agriculture has troubles peculiar to itself. But it shares one difficulty with other industries. It is labour. Yet it would be fatal to think that the agricultural problem is, in this respect, identical with the industrial problem, or to attempt to apply to both exactly the same solutions. The cultivation of the soil is the oldest of our industries, and those who pursue it as their ancestral calling have, in the course of centuries, developed habits of mind that survive from generation to generation. No such complications affect our factories. They are comparatively recent growths. Of the methods of production that they have supplanted little, if anything, survives. With the extinction of the domestic handicraftsmen disappeared the ideals, customs, and traditions of their trades. In the case of cultivators of the soil it is different. The agricultural worker of to-day is a wage-earner, a hired labourer. The system under which he toils is altered. But he tills the same soil by the same processes under the same seasons. At heart he retains the native instincts, ideals, and traditions of the peasant of the eighteenth century, who was either a small farmer, or not exclusively dependent for his home and his livelihood on the sale of his labour on the land at competitive wages. In that direction may perhaps lie the path to contentment and stability. A permanent interest in the land that he cultivates or a share in the produce that he raises, rather than successive increases in cash wages, may prove the remedy for his unrest.

From the standpoint of the twentieth century there are chapters in the story of the agricultural worker which can scarcely be read without indignation. The rack and the dungeon of the Tudors are to us not more inconceivable than the callous inhumanity of the criminal law in the days of the Regent. The best, and the worst, that can be said for these instruments of brutality is that they did not outrage the public opinion of the time. Agricultural workers were not singled out for special treatment. Nor do cases of harshness and oppression tell the whole story. Myriads of acts of fair-play and justice, of human sympathy and neighbourly friendliness, which are not recorded in history, and do not appear on the face of legal documents, must be taken into account before we can form any accurate estimate of rural conditions.

Agricultural Workers in 1800 and 1925

From the fifteenth century onwards, an agricultural and economic change had been in slow, continuous progress. It was the passage from the occupation of the land by groups of occupiers in common to its occupation by individuals. Operating by the enclosure of common fields and the commons which were their adjuncts, it gradually transformed the medieval peasant into the tenant farmer and agricultural worker of to-day. By 1815, the process was practically completed under the pressure of improvements in farming methods, industrial expansion, the growth of new urban centres, and, during the French wars, the menace of famine. Inelastic, adapted only to a stationary population, obstacles to agricultural progress, village farms offered little employment to surplus numbers. Close, self-supporting communities, they produced scanty food beyond the immediate needs of the occupiers themselves. Large tracts of land were withdrawn from their most productive use. Meanwhile, as has been already stated, the cry for food rose more and more loudly from new industrial centres, and, at a later stage, was swollen by the panic-stricken clamour of a nation at war. If only free play could be given to modern methods of production, new resources and improvements had been tested by farmers which promised to supply, and did in fact supply, the national demand for bread and meat. In these considerations lies the economic justification for enclosures.

To weigh the national advantages against the national losses consequent on the change would be a difficult task. Nor can it be safely asserted that action, taken under the sanction of the law in a Parliament where interested landowners exercised a predominant influence, was always and in each individual case morally justified. But it is impossible to find any general evidence of wholesale injustice, still less of robbery. The point has become one of such supreme importance, that it is necessary to consider the procedure by which enclosures were effected and the objects at which they aimed.

During the eighteenth century, enclosures were carried out by private Acts of Parliament; after 1801, by a General Enclosure Act. The proceedings were high-handed, as they always are when compulsory measures are adopted; compulsion is only a " blessed " word in the mouths of those who set it in motion. They began with a petition to enclose a specified area, signed by a majority in values of the persons interested. It was not necessary that the signatories should be a majority in number, and it is probable that, in nearly every instance, the numerical majority of occupiers would have been opposed to change. On receipt of the petition, by leave of the House of Commons, a Private Bill was introduced, read a first and a second time, and referred to a Committee. The Committee received counter-petitions, heard evidence, and reported to the House that the original petition had or had not been substantiated, and that the requisite majority had or had not signed. On this Report the House either rejected the Bill, or read it a third time and passed it. When the Bill received the sanction of the Upper House, it became an Act. Commissioners were appointed, who visited the locality, surveyed and valued the land, and distributed it in compact blocks of freehold among those who proved their title. Their decisions on value were final, but an appeal to the law courts seems to have been allowed on questions of title.

The object of enclosure was not to effect any

transfer of ownership. The men who proved themselves to be owners emerged from the process as owners. In its immediate effect, enclosure rather tended to increase than to diminish the number of freeholders, for it recognized, in certain cases, the claim of copyholders, leaseholders and squatters to a freehold interest in land. What it did was to change the subject-matter of the property owned, to substitute a compact block of freehold land for common rights, and to make the change compulsory. The general principle of enclosure was to recognize the claims of all occupiers of land and commoners who could establish a permanent independent right. Thus, a freeholder, or an owner of a cottage to which common rights were attached received a block of land estimated to be of the same value as his bundle of scattered strips in the common fields or his rights of user of the arable or pasture commons. On the other hand, the claims of those occupiers whose title was only temporary and derivative were not admitted. Thus men who occupied land or privileged cottages only as tenants received no allotment.

The importance of the point justifies two illustrations, one taken from the beginning, the other from the end of the last period of enclosure. In 1767, 988 acres of common fields and commons were enclosed at Steeple Aston in Oxfordshire. The award sets out not only the area allotted to each owner, but the area which each had previously owned in the common fields. Land was allotted to the twenty-three persons who established their legal claims. The following are instances. The Lord of the Manor, Sir C. Cottrell Dormer, owned "3¾ yardlands and 4 'oddlands' and commons thereto belonging." He was allotted 63 acres, 1 rood, 29 perches. Lucy Buswell, "in lieu of 4½ yardlands and commons thereto belonging," received 84 acres, 1 rood, 6 perches. Robert George, "in lieu of 1 yardland and commons belonging," received 21 acres, 3 roods, 21 poles. John Clary, "in lieu of ⅓ yardland and commons belonging," was allotted 3 acres, 1 rood, 4 poles. Eliza Davis "in lieu of 2¾ yardlands with commons belonging," received 53 acres, 2 roods, 7 poles. It may be noted that one leaseholder and one cottager were recognized as owners. The other illustration is taken from the Return of the Enclosure Commissioners given in their Annual Report for 1876. Between the years 1845-75, 590,000 acres were enclosed. They were divided among "25,930 persons. . . . 620 lords of manors received, on an average, 44½ acres each ; 21,810 common-right owners received, on an average, 24 acres each ; 3,500 purchasers (of land sold to pay the expenses of enclosure) received, on an average, 10 acres each." Among the 21,810 common-right owners were 6,624 "shopkeepers and tradesmen, labourers and miners."

Abundant evidence exists to prove that, under the Enclosure Acts, a very large area of land was distributed among a great number of small owners in compact blocks. If the owners could have been protected against themselves in the enjoyment of their properties, and if larger provision had been made for cases in which the exercise of common rights rested on no legal basis, the social and moral injury done by enclosures might have been very greatly mitigated.

The concluding stages of the agricultural change were reached at a most difficult crisis. In many parts of the country, even without enclosures, the old rural organization must probably have broken down under the declining fertility of the land, and

Agricultural Workers in 1800 and 1925

the disappearance of the domestic handicrafts and local industries which were migrating to the new industrial centres of the North. In the South and West of England, the heritage of this transfer of industry was the creation of an unemployed population which forced down the wages of agricultural labour. Everywhere, manufacture and agriculture were simultaneously reorganized on those commercial lines which facilitated increased production at reduced cost. Farming ceased to be a subsistence and became a trade. The united effect of the two reorganizations was to sweep away many small freeholders, tenant farmers, and commoners, who had lived by the cultivation or use of land in combination with the practice of domestic handicrafts. Their places were taken by the large corn-growing, meat-producing farms which met the needs and fashion of the day. The organization of the village, in which wealth and poverty, employer and employed, were almost imperceptibly graded into one another, was broken up. With the destruction of the primitive framework went the traditions of the peasant, his inherited ideals, his ancestral customs, his habitual solutions of the problems of existence. The village was not idyllic. "Auburn" never existed. But in each of these small self-supporting communities, the members lived tranquil, sequestered lives. They enjoyed some degree of independence. They knew few changes beyond those of the recurrent seasons. They rarely took any interest in the world outside their own parish. They were not forced to face the struggle of competition. They bought so little that fluctuations in prices did not disturb their minds ; almost all the simple necessaries of food, drink, and clothing were produced at home. Such conditions of self-supporting isolation can never be exactly reproduced in this crowded country and bustling century.

In unenclosed districts there was little or no demand for hired labour on the land except at harvest. Small freeholders, small farmers, as well as the occupiers of the intermixed strips of the common fields, worked their holdings themselves with the aid of their families. The live-stock was tended by the village shepherd, cowherd, and swineherd. Nor did their style of farming tend to create employment. There were no quickset hedges to trim, or plash or weed. Roots were not grown. There were no drilled crops to clean. There were no stall-fed cattle to tend. Nor, finally, did the common-field farm afford any opening to new-comers to acquire land. It is to causes like these that the extremely slow increase of the rural population up to the end of the eighteenth century must be attributed.

In one direction only was it possible to obtain an interest in the use of land. The common was the pasture of the village farm, and as such was an essential integral adjunct to each arable holding. But rights of grazing and of cutting fuel were also attached to certain cottages, or might be acquired by encroachment if the trespasser was undisturbed for sixty years. Where an owner occupied one of these privileged cottages, he enjoyed common rights as an owner. Where he was only a tenant, he enjoyed them as a tenant, and in consideration of the higher rent which he paid. On enclosure, the claim of the owner, not of the tenant, would be recognized. The number of these privileged cottages was often considerable. At Stanwell, for instance, where 2,126 acres were distributed under an award in 1789, " near 100 " occupiers of cottages claimed common rights. Of these claims, 66 were recognized, and 40 owners were compensated by allotments of land varying from a quarter of an acre to over an acre. Twenty-six of the 66 cottages belonged to two individuals. It would, therefore, appear that, out of the 100 claims 34 were altogether disallowed, probably because, as squatters, the claimants had been in occupation too short a time to establish a legal title.

It was here that enclosures, however sound the legal principle on which they proceeded, often inflicted real hardships. A number of persons, no doubt, were attracted to commons by the facilities which they afforded to a life of comparative idleness, or, to use Defoe's phrase, of "lazy diligence." On the other hand, to many saving and industrious men commons were of inestimable value. They provided free fuel and a run for stock to those who practised domestic handicrafts, and, at certain seasons, hired themselves out as labourers on the land. To them the common was a ladder of thrift. Even if the use they had enjoyed was admitted as the exercise of a legal right and recognized by an allotment of land, the compensation was very frequently inadequate. On the other hand, generosity to men of this type was only possible at the expense of those whose claim to the land had been established at law. To take the case of Steeple Aston, Lucy Buswell, Eliza Davis, Robert George, John Clary, and the other eighteen participants would have complained at least as loudly as Sir C. Cottrell Dormer, if their shares had been reduced in order to create allotments for persons who could show no legal title.

During the greater part of the French War, the full consequences of the recent changes were to some extent concealed. It was a period of distress, less felt, in all probability, in the districts where the food was produced than in the new industrial centres. Rural employment was brisk. The poorest soils were brought into cultivation for food. All available labour was used and paid for at enhanced rates. Calculations of wages in the eighteenth and nineteenth centuries are, at best, approximations. Yet it is evident that between 1790 and 1813 a substantial rise took place. It may not be possible to accept the statements of Arthur Young and of Tooke as absolutely reliable for all parts of the country. But they are in agreement that, between those dates, agricultural wages had " about doubled." Meanwhile the prices of provisions approximately trebled. Bread was so scarce that, if universal famine was to be avoided, rigid economy was needed. High prices were effective weapons against waste, and the Government dared not, as they did in the recent war, lay them aside by subsidizing the loaf at the expense of taxpayers. But they supplemented wages out of the rates by allowances both of money and of bread. By this assistance, by the rise in wages, and by the sustained demand for agricultural labour, the effects of enclosures were temporarily obscured. It was the ebb in the tide of activity that revealed the full results.

The years 1814-36 were the blackest period in the history of the agricultural worker. The depth of misery into which he then fell is the measure of the advance that he has subsequently made. Distress was universal. The war was over ; but " Peace and Plenty " proved a ghastly mockery. Large tracts of arable land fell out of cultivation ; considerable areas were even untenanted. Less and less labour was required. Wages fell to pre-war

Agricultural Workers in 1800 and 1925

levels ; but even at the lowered rates, work was hard
to find and harder still to keep. Unemployment
was not confined to the land. The reduction to a
peace footing of the Army and Navy and of the
store, commissariat and transport departments threw
thousands of men out of employment. Industries
which the war had stimulated to unnatural activity,
languished. The introduction of machinery into
manufacturing processes displaced crowds of manual
workers. Over-production glutted the impoverished
markets of the export trade, and checked the revival
and expansion of industry. Everywhere there was
a fierce struggle for work and wages.

Into this strange swirl of competition agricultural
workers were plunged, when once the shelter of the
self-sufficing village was disturbed. The effect of
the rural changes was now brought home with
tremendous force. The sale of their labour on the
land had become the workers' only means of livelihood. The domestic handicrafts which supplemented
their earnings had been swept into manufacturing
centres, where they supplied wages to thousands
of artisans. The land which provided their food
and fuel and fed their live-stock was turned into a
factory of bread and meat for the towns. All that
they had formerly produced for themselves, they
now had to buy. They felt the full pressure of
prices, and the lower their wages, the keener the
pinch.

The evil consequences of the short-sighted humanity which, during the war, had levelled the barriers
of the Poor Law, completed the ruin of the rural
population. Wages had been supplemented by allowances paid out of the rates, and proportioned
to the size of a man's family and the price of the
quartern loaf. If wages fell below the subsistence

Pauper Dependence

level, the deficiency was made good by the ratepayer. Bound, if necessary, to defray the whole cost of the able-bodied poor, the parish gladly accepted from an employer any weekly payment, however small, which partially relieved the charge on the rates. Thus a mass of temporary labour, subsidized, and therefore cheap, was created and made available for the cultivation of the land. To many of the men pauper dependence was a thing to be resented as a disgrace and a curse. But however anxious they might be to support themselves by permanent work, and so to preserve their independence, they were powerless. They were undersold by the rate-subvented labour. To others the security of sub-sistence, the light labour, the opportunities for idleness, made a pauper's life attractive.

The demoralization spread far and wide. It overran the South ; it extended to the Midlands ; it crept towards the North. Had the abuses of pauperism lasted a few years longer, a generation might have sprung up which knew no other exis-tence, and were strangers to the fine traditions and sturdy independence of their forefathers. From that danger the country was saved, partly by the self-respecting pride of men of the older stamp, partly by the wiser administration of the law which pre-vailed in many districts, partly by legislative reform, and partly by the reviving prosperity of the industry. Before 1836 the progressive deterioration had been arrested. It had touched bottom. Out of the depths the upward climb began.

The advance was neither even nor rapid. Agri-culture underwent many vicissitudes of fortune, and, as a consequence, the progress of agricultural workers suffered more than one set-back. But, as compared with 1814-36, their advance has been

65 5

continuous ; they have never looked back. For years the odds were against them. Isolated from one another in remote country districts, commanding no capital beyond their labour, living in chronic poverty, generally in debt to the village tradesmen, dependent on their employers for both home and wages, agricultural labourers were far less capable of protecting themselves than were the artisans in the towns. Immobile, uneducated, voteless, and therefore without political influence, they found it difficult to combine and, without combination, impossible to bargain. In the agricultural prosperity of the sixties and the early seventies, they had in some districts to some extent shared. If statistics of wages can be at all relied upon, their average earnings in 1872 had nearly doubled as compared with 1820. But in the South and West the excess of the demand for employment over the supply told against them heavily.

The year 1872 stands out as a landmark in the record of progress. One winter evening (February 7) nearly a thousand men gathered at Wellesbourne in Warwickshire to listen to one of themselves, known for miles round as a skilled hedge-cutter and a local preacher. The speaker was Joseph Arch. It was a dark night, and lanterns, swung from bean poles, shed a feeble light on the scene. Mounted on a pig-stool, set under a chestnut tree, Arch looked down on a sea of upturned faces, over which flickered the uncertain gleams of the swaying lanterns. In his mind, steeped in the imagery and phraseology of the Bible, he likened his audience to the children of Israel, " with the darkness all about them . . . waiting for some one to lead them out of the land of Egypt." The outcome of the meeting was the decision to form a union. The men demanded 2s. 8d. a day ; hours 6 to 5, except on Saturday, when they were to be 6 to 3 ; and 4d. an hour overtime. Little notice seems to have been taken of their demand, and in March they struck. Public sympathy with their action was aroused ; Archibald Forbes, fresh from his triumphs in the Franco-Prussian War, pleaded their cause in the Press ; considerable sums were subscribed for their support. After three months, they won a partial victory. Wages were advanced—in some cases to the 16s. which had been demanded.

At the height of its prosperity the Union mustered 70,000 members. From being purely economic, it became largely political in its scope. Many sympathisers were alienated by fear of its ultimate objects. During the great lock-out of 1874, which lasted eighteen weeks in the Eastern Counties, this loss of public support contributed to the ultimate defeat of the National Union. It never recovered the blow, and dwindled into insignificance. It had not altogether failed. It won the vote for the agricultural worker ; it obtained some slight advance in wages ; it demonstrated the possibility of combination on a large scale ; it relieved the congestion of agricultural labour by emigrating, between 1873 and 1881, some 700,000 persons.* But, during the twenty years of agricultural depression with which the nineteenth century closed, no expansion of the upward movement could possibly be expected. As prices dropped, wages fell. Land passed out of cultivation. Thousands of men were only kept in employment by the kindly feeling of employers, who were themselves tottering on the verge of bankruptcy. From 1896 onwards,

* The figures were given by Arch in his evidence before the Royal Commission in 1881 (Parl. Papers, 1882, Vol. XIV., p. 51).

the tide was turning and the industry beginning to revive. Wages crept upwards, following the gradual rise of prices. In 1914 the weekly earnings of adult male labourers in England, not being men in charge of animals, may have approximately averaged 20s. But in many counties the rates were far lower. An Oxfordshire labourer, in receipt of 15s. 3d. or less, found but hungry comfort in an average.

For months before August, 1914, and the outbreak of war, the agitation for an advance in wages, shorter hours, and a half-holiday was gathering strength. A minimum wage, and the machinery to enforce it, began to be discussed by politicians. In a large number of counties strikes were threatening. Trade Unions promised support to their agricultural brethren. Agriculture had the unenviable reputation of a sweated industry, underpaid and undermanned. With the declaration of war it became evident that, when every pound of food was of value, the risk of prolonged disturbance of labour conditions was not to be lightly faced. It was at first hoped that the demand for labour would enable workers to obtain substantial advances proportioned to rising prices. On this ground the Milner Committee of 1915 had decided not to recommend a minimum wage.

Still the Government hesitated. But the new policy of stimulating production, adopted by the Coalition Government of 1916–18, necessitated the immediate establishment of machinery to deal with wages. The Corn Production Act of 1917 created a Wage Board and fixed, as a starting point, the minimum wage of 25s. a week, which was offered to National Service Volunteers. In fairness to agricultural workers, no other course seemed possible. The Government was making every effort to increase labour on the land, and every additional man or woman weakened the worker's position in bargaining and profiting by the demand for his skill. From the point of view of the agricultural worker, the 400,000 additional workers, women as well as men, whom the Government placed on the land were State-assisted " blacklegs." Nor was the introduction of this mass of subsidized labour the only handicap which the State, in the campaign of food production, imposed on agricultural labourers in their freedom of bargaining for a rise in wages. Many of the men were exempted from military service as being indispensable on particular farms. Every one of these exempted workers knew that, in the event of his dismissal, he would at once become liable for military service. If a Wage Board and a minimum wage was, in the exceptional circumstances of the war, an absolute necessity, the machinery has, in the opinion of many competent judges, justified its modified continuance, in some form or other, under peace conditions. With the end of the war disappeared the need for centralization and uniformity of scale. Agricultural Wages Boards now exist as County Committees, and the wages and conditions that are fixed vary from district to district.

If the general position of the ordinary adult labourer to-day is compared with that which he held in 1800-36, it will be seen to have improved beyond comparison or recognition. Even as compared with 1872 the improvement is striking. To-day the agricultural worker—and, it may be added, his wife—enjoy full rights of citizenship ; they can make their influence felt in the government of their parish, the administration of their county, the direction of the affairs of the Empire. He is no longer isolated from his fellow-workers in remote country districts ; he is, or can become, a member of a dwindling but still efficient organization. He has himself received a free education, and his children are being educated free of cost to himself. His outlook has widened. He can read, and take an intelligent interest in the affairs of the world. Largely at the expense of the nation and of his employer, he is insured against sickness, and can count on a pension in his old age. His industry is no longer overcrowded ; it is on the contrary, if it were prosperous, undermanned. His necessary hours of labour have been shortened by at least 15 hours a week. His wages are in most counties independent of weather conditions. If he chooses, and his employer desires, he can work overtime beyond the 50 hours of summer and 48 hours of winter, at a special rate. He has a half-holiday every week. As compared with 1800, his minimum wages—and his actual wages are often higher— have been more than trebled ; as compared with 1872, they have been, in what were the low-paid counties, approximately doubled. Necessity no longer drives his wife and children to labour in the fields.

The decline in the purchasing power of money has largely discounted the reality of the nominal advance in wages, yet there is a greater margin in favour of the worker after providing the necessities of life. He is better housed than at any previous period in his history. That there is a shortage of cottages is true. But it is in urban and semi-urban areas, and not in agricultural districts that the shortage of accommodation is most serious and the overcrowding most intense. The proportion of insanitary and defective cottages has been greatly reduced. In a great majority of cases, he has a garden or an allotment on which his greater leisure may be profitably bestowed. If he chooses to apply, and can satisfy the moderate requirements of the local authority, he has a chance of a small holding. Finally, the health conditions in which he lives are superior to those of urban populations. The Returns of the Registrar-General for 1911 and 1912 prove that this superiority is maintained at all ages of childhood up to the age of 15, and at all subsequent ages up to 70—with one exception. That exception is phthisis between the ages of 20 and 25, and the Registrar-General explains it by the number of young unmarried persons who return to their rural homes having contracted the disease under urban conditions.

Yet contentment has not been attained. It cannot be reached by pressing too far the analogy between agriculture and other industries. There are important differences. A farm has no tally or check-weigher, no roof, no clock, no artificial light, no nerve-racking conditions of employment. On the farm there exist no means of measuring the output of labour. The land is unprotected against rain and frost ; its cultivation depends on weather conditions, and for weeks together in the winter months there is not work enough to keep the staff fully employed. On a farm, the men cannot be marked in and out at the beginning and end of the day, as they can be, and are, at the gate of a factory. In a factory, hours of labour can be made uniform by artificial light ; on the land, they must, of necessity, vary. In a factory, the working hours are a time of concentrated strain, often spent under nerve-exhausting conditions ; on the land, if, at certain seasons, the hours are inevitably longer, they are less exhausting, both physically and nervously. Between agricultural and industrial problems there are essential differences which are necessarily reflected in rates of wages.

Nor will contentment be reached by exclusive reliance on such mechanical methods of determining differences as Wage Boards. A machine is a sorry substitute for the fine agricultural tradition of friendliness and confidence which prevailed, and still prevails, between the best employers and their men. Every agricultural community has to live, work, and do business together. At every turn the human touch is needed. Each section has responsibilities towards the other which it cannot evade by sheltering behind a union, an organizer, or a Wage Board. It is by standing together, and not by dividing apart into contending camps, that employers and employed will best reach that contentment which lies at the root of a prosperous agriculture.

CHAPTER V

On our country villages, the effect of enclosures can rather be traced in the life than in the form. The shell remains ; the kernel has shrivelled.

Behind some of our older villages lie more than fifteen centuries of history. Yet of the three factors in the agricultural industry—land, capital, and man—the human element has been least studied. Better farming and better business have engrossed more attention . than better living. In towns, civilization in all its manifold forms has swept onwards, leaving the country a century behind. To the citizen the rural population is a mystery ; he scarcely conceives of rural interests as human interests. He thinks most of cheap food. Yet, before many years have passed, it will possibly be recognized that there is no more important influence on national life than the wife of the rural worker, no more important home than her cottage, no more important social need than that of bringing the conditions of country living into line with the development of the towns.

In the United States and in every part of re-constituted Europe, rural life is the subject of discussion, if not of legislation. In this country,

of recent years, efforts have been made to give
our villages a fuller existence, to break down the
apathy which is bred of limited opportunities and of
an admirable but almost fatalistic patience, to
revive something of their ancient gaiety, to render
life less solitary and more attractive, to show that
all the real prizes of human happiness do not
necessarily lie at a distance from the land. Much
more is needed than amusements or even increased
mental occupations. But they are something, and
it is to be hoped that, before it is too late, and
in spite of agricultural depression, these efforts
may be increasingly successful. Unless decay can
be arrested, it is not creditable to twentieth-century
progress that national life should be rotting at its
vital roots.

For lovers of the country its villages have a
peculiar fascination. But it is a dispiriting reflection that, albeit in dependence, squalor, poverty,
and insanitary conditions, medieval villages enjoyed
a fullness of corporate and individual interest which,
compared with to-day, is as a flowing river to a
stagnant pond. The loss of interest and of variety
is largely due to the break-up of the village farm.
On the features of remote clusters of inhabitants
is still stamped each stage in social and economic
history, from the distant days when land was
everything and trade nothing, down to the present
century when, as pessimists assure us, agriculture
is going to the devil in a gale of wind. Some in one
direction, some in another, they present impressions
of the past so vividly that the old world seems to
be still kept in living touch with the new. The
evidences which any one village affords of ancient
habits, customs and manners is fragmentary ; but
facts and details collected over ever-widening areas

may enable competent scholars, in the near future, to recapture the life of our forefathers with an increased degree of freshness and completeness.

In many of our villages the signs of extreme antiquity are unmistakable. They do not force themselves on the eye by glaring contrasts of medieval buildings with modern erections. Rather the long passage of time has mellowed the whole into a harmony of unobtrusive colouring, and steeped it in the pervasive atmosphere of age. Nowhere is the old-world character more faithfully preserved than in the features of hamlets on the slopes of the Downs. Here are found some of the oldest sites of villages, and for obvious reasons. It was on the edges of the Downs that the least labour told the most, and that the transition from the nomadic life of pastoral hordes to more settled agricultural communities was the easiest. Fertile valleys, tangled with forest growth, remained uncleared when dry and comparatively treeless uplands were occupied and cultivated. To these chalk escarpments, with their wide, bare pastures and sheltered dips, were attracted not only the Saxon settlers, but the more ancient inhabitants of the country. The uplands were grazed by flocks and herds, while the steep sides, or the pockets of soil below the rise, were scratched up for scanty patches of corn. Nor did the Downs serve agricultural purposes only. They were the sites of mysterious megalithic monuments. They were camps and battlegrounds and burying places. They were also natural highways. In districts along the lines of the Downs it was a common tradition that, on quiet nights, could still be heard the tramp of armed hosts and the creak of their heavy chariots as they passed from camp to camp along the ancient tracks.

Country Villages

In its physical aspects, East Hendred, in Berkshire, may be taken as a typical Down village, following the uniform plan that our forefathers stamped on the face of the uplands of South-Eastern England. The shape of the parish is that of a long-sided parallelogram, running north to south. The northern and north-western base follows the course of a stream; the southern base, high up on the Downs themselves, meets and rests on the boundaries of other parishes. Between the two long eastern and western sides is the land, cultivated, grazed, or mown by the occupiers, and adapted to the various needs of a self-supporting, self-sufficing community. At the southern end stretched the wide grazing grounds of the Downs. At the northern and north-western extremity, where the brook turned the corn-mills, the best of the land was chosen for the meadows; the poorer parts afforded the rough pasture, mixed with bush, small wood, bracken, and rushes, that are suggested by the field names of Band's Moor, Long Moor, Great and Little Moor, Mill Moor, Picked Moor, Further and Upper Moor. The arable land lay on the drier portions, pushing upwards to the slope of the hills, until the soil became too thin and poor for cultivation. According to this uniform arrangement, the Downs were never ploughed. It would therefore almost seem that the horizontal terraces on the hills, which are a prominent feature of the country, and are popularly known as "daisses," "lynches," or "lynchets," were the work of hill-folk at a stage of husbandry more primitive than that of the Saxon settlers.

The arable land is the "land of Ceres." Here were grown, in unvarying triennial succession, the crops "of wheat, rye, barley, vetches, oats, and

Unchanged Aspects

peas," which Shakespeare exhaustively enumerates in a line from *The Tempest*. The appearance of the land under the plough preserves some of the features which it bore in the days of the Plantagenets. It is still a bare, hedgeless, and, but for recent plantations, treeless expanse, with none of the small enclosures or detached isolated farmhouses which generally mark individual occupation and modern farming. A prophet of the seventeenth century foretold that " thorn and horn will make England forlorn," or, in other words, that pasture fields enclosed by hedges, and stock-farming, would strip England of her rural population. East Hendred has so far escaped these dangers. It has remained a corn-growing district, and such divisions as are made between the broad arable fields are not made by thorn hedges, but by the grass-grown banks, " balks " or " meares " of medieval farmers. To-day the iron plough traverses the land, drawn by the untiring arm of steam. But the great hedgeless expanse makes it easy to conjure up a picture of the teams of eight oxen, plodding slowly to and fro over the patchwork pattern of acre and half-acre strips, dragging behind them the cumbrous plough with its wooden mould-boards, as in the days of Crecy or of Agincourt.

Towards the northern and north-western boundary of the parish, at no great distance from, but above, the stream, stands the village. In it are gathered practically all the population. Though the danger of isolation and the need for combined defence have passed away, detached farmhouses and cottages are still almost as rare as they were in Norman times. Surrounded by the wide expanse of meadow, arable pasture, and moorland, the occupiers clustered round the church and manor house for mutual help and protection in this world and the next. The village was laid out on no plan. It grew. Straight lines are rare. Nothing shows its natural growth more clearly than the labyrinth of winding lanes which saunter from one homestead to another. Apparently engineered on the medieval principle, dear alike to politician and road-maker, that one good or bad turn deserves another, their direction is mostly governed by ancient enclosures of individual occupiers. One lane called "Cat Street" commemorates St. Catharine, on whose festival was held one of the two annual fairs, abandoned three centuries ago. Two others, Ford Lane and King Lane, leading to one of the mills, strike towards the stream with the purposeful directness of public utility.

Timber-framed, straw-thatched, or tile-roofed, most of the houses belong to Tudor times. But they have displaced the mud-built, earth-floored, single-roomed, one-storied, chimney-less structures which sheltered the families and the live-stock of the earlier settlers. Bishop Hall's picture of the interior of the home of the Elizabethan copyholder, with its outside walls of timber uprights and cross-beams, forming raftered panels daubed with clay or cob, was at least true of three previous centuries:

> Of one bay's breadth, God wot, a silly cote
> Whose thatched spars are furred with sluttish soote,
> A whole inch thick, shining like blackmoor's brows
> Through smoke that through the headlesse barrel blows ;
> At his bed's feete feeden his stalled teame,
> His swine beneath, his pullen o'er the beam.

Otherwise the changes have been slight. From early times, orchards and gardens, in which to grow fruit and such green vegetables as were then known, and mostly beans, were essential to the health of a population living largely on meat and fish in salted form. Nor was it long before the open-field farmers had fenced in their tofts and crofts—tiny yards for their ricks and stacks, as well as small enclosures of grass for rearing calves, or for the working oxen which could not endure to " labour all day, and then to be put to the commons or before the herdsmen."

East Hendred has not been associated with events of national importance. It has given birth to no one conspicuous in history. Yet it possesses one rare feature which, it may not be fanciful to think, intensifies the pervasive charm of its old-world atmosphere. The village has known no complete severance from the Church of the Middle Ages. A portion of the people always adhered to the older faith. The parish church is, of course, in Protestant hands. But, in a free chapel, attached to the ancient home of the Eystons, services of the Roman Catholic Church have been held with remarkable continuity. Built between 1253 and 1291, and dedicated, in a quaint order of dedication, to St. Amand and St. John the Baptist, it lost its endowments at the Dissolution of the Monasteries. But the chapel itself remained. In 1688 it was desecrated, probably rather from wantonness than by the order of any responsible authority. The story is told in a manuscript volume, addressed to his " Deare Children," by Charles Eyston (1667-1721), the " great friend and acquaintance " of Thomas Hearne, and himself known in the family as the "antiquary." At Hungerford, in December, 1688, the Prince of Orange had met the Commissioners of James II. His troops, on their way from that town to Oxford, passed over the Golden Mile, the turf road which runs along the eastern border of East Hendred.

Some loose fellowes (whether by orders or not I cannot tell) came hyther, went into the Chappell, pretended to mock the priest by supping out of the Chalice, which they would have taken away

Country Villages

had it been silver, as they themselves afterwards gave out ; however, having torn down the JESUS MARIA from the Altar, which holy names were painted upon Pannells in the same Frames, where the JESUS MARIA are now wrought in Bugles, they retired, taking an old suite of Church stuffe with them to Oxford, where they dress up a mawkin with it and set it up there on the Topp of a Bon-Fyre. This happened on Monday, December the 11th, 1688, and this is all the mischief they did, besides breaking the lamp and carrying away the Sanctus bell.

In other respects East Hendred has not differed from other villages in the development of its social and economic life. Every medieval village was a small world to itself. Means of communication with neighbours were few, and rarely used. Each village produced almost all that it needed. It consumed the food that it grew. Except salt and iron, it bought little, and that little by barter. Coin seldom changed hands. But isolation had its dangers. Too weak to enforce the law, the central government was powerless to safeguard the enterprise, the property, or even the life of individuals. A small man could not stand alone ; unprotected, he tempted violence. With less personal freedom and independence than the towns, rural communities were similarly organized for mutual protection and responsibility. Municipal charters, guilds merchant and trade guilds, stood between individual citizens and oppression. In a somewhat similar way the organization of the manor protected individual villagers. The lord might be, perhaps often was, a domestic tyrant ; but at least he shielded his tenants from the rapacity of others. Nor did his powers, even over the unfree, long remain entirely arbitrary. The rights which he exercised, the services that he exacted, were gradually defined and regulated by customs of which the occupiers of the land, as judges, witnesses, or jurors of the Manorial Courts, were themselves the guardians.

Home Occupations

Behind the door of the peasants, few gleams of light penetrate. Of their public merrymakings, generally under the auspices of the Church, we know much : of their daily shifts for food we hear little or nothing. As each cereal year drew to its close, the store of food dwindled. Experience taught our ancestors to " eat within the tether." But many must never have learned to " spare at the brink and not at the bottom." Harvests were, therefore, not merely picturesque scenes of bustle and effort ; they meant also the temporary return of plenty. There were scenes of feasting, none the less cheerful because the people knew that famine trode hard at its heels. If the village farmers ever touched fresh butcher's meat, it was only in the autumn when the cattle came off the aftermath of the meadows and the stubble of the arable land.

For home occupations neither men nor women were ever at a loss. Most of the rude utensils for domestic use and the implements employed in agriculture were home-made. Such, for instance, were the beechen bowls, platters and spoons, and there were always horn-mugs to rivet or leather jugs to patch. Out of wood the men cut and fixed handles to their tools, fashioned ox-yokes, and bows, forks, racks and rack-staves, shaped and hardened the teeth for the rakes from ash or willow, plaited reeds into baskets or osiers into traces, cut the flails from thorn or holly and fastened them with leathern thongs to the staves. Women spun and wove wool into cloth or hemp or nettles into linen. They plaited straw or reeds for neck-collars, stuffed and stitched sheep-skin bags for the cart saddles, peeled rushes and made candles. Their spinning-wheels, distaffs and needles were always busy. They brewed as well as baked for their households. Summer and winter, neither men nor women were idle, and they worked at least as much for themselves as for a master.

Of the economic life of peasants in the medieval village, the records of manorial administration supply many details. Few general statements can be made to which exceptions may not be found. Yet in the midst of endless variations the trend of development is uniform. In all the records, and the Court Rolls of the Manor of the Eystons at East Hendred here and there confirm the truth of the statement, may be traced a movement towards personal freedom, and, up to a certain point, towards a firmer hold upon the land.

The group of persons who were gathered within the bounds of rural manors were, in the most literal sense of the word and to a peculiar degree, communities. Externally cut off from the outside world, their dwellings not scattered but huddled together, they were united in a singularly close relationship. Their farming, on which all depended for daily food, was their common enterprise. Each individual took the produce of his own holding, but the whole body of partners cultivated the ploughland collectively. Their arable lots lay in strips intermixed with those of their neighbours ; they co-operated in their labours for the Lord of the Manor ; they grazed the pastures in common ; they shared the meadows, often annually by lot ; when the hay and corn were cleared, their combined flocks and herds roamed over the land together. In the tithings, in which all were enrolled, the members were responsible for the behaviour of one another. In the Manor Courts the tenants gathered, many of them, when documentary evidence begins, still distinguished only by such local identifications as

The Manor Courts

Richard atte Lane, John le Longe, Peter le Fraunk, Thomas atte Grene, Roger atte Wode, William atte Watere, meeting as judges, jurors, suitors, or witnesses, to assist in the regulation of their economic and social life. The degree of external isolation and of internal unity, interdependence, and mutual responsibility, in which they stood to one another, may have stunted enterprise and starved opportunity. But, for good as well as evil, it allowed no room for the exaggerated individualism and feverish competition of modern life.

Efficiency in so complex an organization as a rural manor required careful account-keeping and frequent meetings of the Manor Courts for the discharge of their miscellaneous business. The receipts and payments for which the steward or bailiff accounts were extremely various. But here their interest lies mainly in the light that they throw on the advance of the unfree tenants towards practical freedom. The wages bill of the lord of a medieval manor, whether his land still lay in intermixed strips in the open fields or was consolidated into a compact Home Farm, was extremely small. His bond-tenants supplied the team-labour and most of the manual labour. At one period, they, their services, and all that they possessed, had been, really as well as theoretically, at his will and mercy. They were bound to the land ; their live-stock could be distrained to meet his debts ; they rendered whatever services he demanded ; they could neither buy nor sell freely ; they were subject to his arbitrary taxation ; they could neither marry their daughters nor apprentice their sons without his licence.

In the eye of the law the position of the bond-tenants might remain unaltered. But before the middle of the thirteenth century custom had modified the severity of legal theory. Rents in money, produce or labour were no longer indeterminate; they had become fixed and certain. The men held land as customary tenants, and were on their way to become copyholders. It was in this position that they stood when, in 1276, the documentary evidence begins at Banstead, in Surrey. Subsequent stages in the advance from personal dependence on the lord to the financial relations of landlord and tenant were accelerated by the Black Death. The pestilence shook the manorial organization to its foundations. Already the process of commuting personal liabilities and services into fixed annual payments had begun. The Survey of the Manor of Banstead in 1325, for instance, shows that the lord had surrendered his right of arbitrary taxation for a fixed yearly " tallage " assessed on the acreage of the holding. After 1349 the process went on apace. Numbers of tenants had been swept away by the Plague ; their empty tenements could not be re-let on the old terms. They either remained void, or they were let on lease and the labour services lost. Fifteen years after the Plague, the accounts show that seventeen holdings stood vacant at Banstead. To supplement the depleted staff, labour had to be hired and its wages paid in cash. Money was provided by commuting into coin a number of services, such as those of malting the lord's barley, carting his timber, hoeing his corn, or the Winter and Lenten ploughings. The form which the transaction takes illustrates the tenacity of the legal theory of serfdom. The labour of the men belongs to their lord ; they buy from him, and he sells to them, the use of their own muscles.

Advance to Personal Freedom

Wages, as the century advanced, continued to rise. The medieval system of farming the demesne had broken down. Without personal superintendence the new method of farming with hired labour could not be made to pay. Large or absentee landowners retired from business, let their demesne lands on lease at yearly rents to tenant farmers, and, no longer needing labour services, accepted the cash equivalents from their copyholders, supplemented by payment of the quit-rents, heriots, and fines on transfer which were sanctioned by the customs registered in the Court Rolls. Naturally these changes advanced at a pace which varied with the conditions of each manor. At East Hendred, in Berkshire, the rate of progress was more leisurely than at Banstead, in Surrey. But the advance was made. In a Court Roll of the Manor of Arches belonging to the Eyston family, is the entry for 1410, that the lord granted his tenants permission to compound for manual labour at the rate of fourpence a man for the day. The relaxation of the old tenures meant an advance towards personal freedom. It meant that money payments had become more valuable to the lord than the number or the muscles of his men. It meant also that the barriers against competition and individualism were crumbling. The strongest and most enterprising begin to lay field to field ; the weakest go to the wall and lose their grip on the land. At Saleby, in Lincolnshire, the manorial accounts at the end of the fifteenth century show that, while, in the aggregate, the fixed money rents remained practically the same as in 1291, they were paid by half the number of tenants. The size of the holding was larger ; the number of holders was smaller. It was not only the lease-holding farmers who were increasing ; the landless class of wage-earners, often itinerant, was multiplying.

So long as the manorial system flourished, the Courts were the centres of its efficiency. In practice the differences between the Court Baron, the customary Court, and the View, at which the tithing-men reported defaults and offences committed within their tithings, were not very strictly observed. In the days of their zenith they were entrusted with wide powers. At East Hendred, the Manor of the Carthusian Priory of Sheen, by express grant from Henry V., possessed criminal jurisdiction, including the privilege of a pillory, a tumbral,* and a gallows for malefactors. Even when no direct authority was conferred, considerable powers were exercised by Manor Courts in criminal and civil cases of minor importance, such as assault, debt, trespass or slander.

The main business arose out of manorial rights and the conditions of the occupation and cultivation of the land. Through the Courts a Lord of the Manor maintained his hold on bondmen. Here their flights were reported, steps ordered for their recovery, or licences paid for their residence outside the Manor. On the other hand, the Courts helped the bondman in his passage to greater freedom. Its records of rents and services first defined his precarious obligations, and then raised him from a customary tenant to a copyholder by copy of the Court Roll. Here were entered the terms of customary tenancies, their surrender, the admission of new tenants, the payments of fines on entry. In 1804

---

* The tumbral, otherwise called a trebuchet, a thewe or a cucking-stool, was a chair in which offenders, mostly women, were fastened. At Lynchmere, in Sussex, the Augustinian Priory had the right of "thurset," *i.e.*, of sentencing to the thewe. The punishment was used for various offences, ranging from adultery to the sale of rotten fish.

The Court Rolls

it is by the "Ancient Court Roll" of the "House of John (sic) of Bethlem of Shine"—two and a half centuries after the Dissolution of the Priory—that the tenants of the King's Manor at East Hendred established their title to copyholds of inheritance on a fine of one year's rent. On the same evidence they also admitted their liability to a heriot of the best animal (or the best goods) belonging to a deceased tenant. Animals were valued by the members of the Court. At East Hendred in 1409 the right to a heriot is in transition from the delivery of the animal itself to the payment of its value. The Court Roll of the Manor of Arches records a heriot of a black horse, due from the estate of a deceased tenant. The animal was valued by the Court at 8s. At this price it was bought back by the heir ; but, as he could not at once find the money, he was allowed to take the horse, depositing as security for the payment a brass dish of the value of 16s.

Other cases before the Courts arose out of obligations of the customary tenants, such as that of keeping their tenements in repair. The flimsy construction of these wattle and daub structures is illustrated by the frequent reports of their ruinous condition, and by the short time allowed to remedy the defects. In the earliest Court Roll at East Hendred (1388) no less than seven tenements are reported to be in a ruinous state. Most numerous of all are the cases in which the tenants enforce against one another, or against strangers, their regulations for the occupation and cultivation of land. Tenants are reported for neglect to repair their portion of the roads and bridges, or the fences and stiles, for which they are individually liable ; for default in scouring dykes and water-courses ;

for turning out more stock than they were entitled to have on the common pastures ; for trespassing with their cattle or sheep on growing crops ; or for encroaching on their neighbours' strips. The Latin of the Court Roll at East Hendred, in which this last offence is recorded, is not classical—" John Hutchins incroachiavit aratro suo " ; but the meaning is clear, and the curse in the Commination Service on the man who moved his neighbour's landmark had a real meaning for medieval farmers.

In the Courts, also, with the tenants as jurors, suitors or witnesses, were regulated many details of social life. Here, for instance, were presented wrangling scolds or tavern-haunters. Idlers were deprived of their holdings and, as a last resort, expelled from the Manor. Fines were imposed for slovenly work at harvest. The necessary contributions were levied for the repair of the stocks or the pound. Millers were fined for mixing rubbish with their flour, bakers for selling short weight, brewers who adulterated their beer, ale-wives or tavern keepers who used false measures or mixed their drink with foreign ingredients, carriers who failed to deliver goods, householders who harboured strangers without a licence. In these and many other matters, the villagers, through the manorial courts, in the days of their effectiveness, had a voice.

In East Hendred there were no less than five Manors, three of which were formed out of estates mentioned in the Domesday Survey—one belonging to the Crown in right of Edward the Confessor, one to the Court of Evreux, the other to Henry de Ferrers. The Royal Manor was given by the Empress Matilda to the Abbey of Reading, and was therefore known as the Abbey Manor. At the Dissolution it was regranted by Henry VIII., and eventually (1623) was bought by the Eystons. The second Manor was granted by Simon Count of Evreux to the Priory of Noyon-sur-Andelle. When, in 1414, the Priory was suppressed as an alien house, the Manor was given by Henry V. to the Carthusian Priory at Sheen, near Richmond. The Priory was highly favoured by the King. To it he granted not only the criminal jurisdiction already noticed, but the privilege of holding a weekly market and a fair twice a year. The Carthusians were not ungrateful. In the village street still stands the disused Chapel of Jesus of Bethlehem, and the house attached to it, which they built shortly after coming into possession. At the Dissolution the Manor passed to the Crown and became known as the King's Manor. Till its sale in 1823, its Stewardship, like that of the Chiltern Hundreds, was used as an office of profit to vacate a seat in Parliament. The third Manor, that of Arches, represents the lands of Henry de Ferrers. It is the only one of the five Manors which has always been in lay hands. It descended by inheritance (1443) to the Eystons, to whom it has ever since belonged. The fourth Manor, that of Framptons, after belonging to the Benedictine Priory of Frampton in Dorsetshire, eventually passed to Sir John Pollen. The fifth Manor, popularly known as New College Manor, belonged to the Benedictine Priory for Nuns at Littlemore in Oxfordshire, and after the Dissolution, to Lord Williams of Thame. He left it (1559) with other property, to endow the Almshouse and Free Grammar School which he founded at Thame. As trustees of the benefaction it was vested in the Warden and Scholars of New College, from whom its name is derived.

Eight centuries of history are spanned, and

Country Villages

Domesday Book is linked to the Ordnance Survey, by the local names of buildings or of fields which preserve the memory of four out of the five Manors. Their existence in the same area, in theory, complicates the management of the commonable lands. The sense of the community probably suggested a practical solution. Thus a Court Roll of the Manor of Arches in 1674 records an arrangement by which the tenants met those of the King's Manor for the purpose of setting out " meare-stones " (*i.e.*, boundaries). Whether the multitude of manors conduced to early freedom it is impossible to say. The number of copyholders is large. On the King's Manor in 1650, there were twenty-one copyholders to one tenant in free socage. A somewhat similar proportion existed on the lay Manor of Arches. The form of tenure was also secure. Except by their own act, copyholders of inheritance, with fixed fines, held the land almost as firmly as freeholders. Both classes are equally described as yeomen.

By the middle of the sixteenth century serfdom and labour services had practically disappeared. Yet, so long as village farms survived, the relations of the occupiers to one another remained the same as at the Conquest. More and more of the intermixed strips of arable land might, through exchange or purchase, be consolidated in the hands of individuals. But, where the framework was intact, a large proportion of the population remained partners in the common enterprise, and most of the arable land was still cultivated in open-fields.

East Hendred, like other Down villages, was little affected by the extensive conversion of arable land to pasture, which, in the sixteenth century, broke up so many open-field farms. Neither of the principal

causes which elsewhere promoted the enclosing
movement were urgent among the Berkshire Downs.
In some districts, centuries of incessant cropping,
combined with shortage of manure, had so impoverished the soil that it could only recover under grass.
But Down farmers to some extent escaped this
danger ; chalk, easily accessible at their doors,
provided them with a natural means of maintaining
and restoring fertility. In many districts, also,
pasture was so scarce that, without laying ploughland to grass, farmers could not increase their sheep
or profit by the prosperity of the wool trade. Here,
too, Down villages had the advantage. Their pastures were abundant enough to remove the temptation to abandon corn. They were thus comparatively untouched by the first wave of enclosure
which rose in other districts to the height of revolution.

Already notable among Berkshire villages for its
flocks of sheep, East Hendred remained a corn-
growing open-field village. For one brief period,
1450-1560, it turned from agriculture to trade.
All round it the clothier industry was thriving.
East Hendred, with its weekly market, its two fairs,
and its home-produced wool, might well hope to
share in the prosperity. It set up its fulling mill ;
it had its terraces for drying cloth ; a brass in the
parish church commemorates a clothier family ;
three East Hendred litigants at the end of the
fifteenth century are described respectively as a
" Kerseyman," a " Clothman," and a " Chapman."
But, except as a domestic handicraft, the industry
never became established. Perhaps the water-
power proved insufficient. With this brief interlude
of commercial ambition, the village resumed its
economic life on agricultural lines.

Country Villages

Unaffected by religious persecution, civil war, or political revolution, the medieval organization of agriculture, where it remained at all, entered on the eighteenth century unaltered. Its crops, its live-stock, its implements, its methods and practices were those of the Middle Ages. In many districts it had been displaced by enclosures carried out in the interest of private persons. Economically, a more productive, as well as more profitable, use was made of the soil by individual occupation than by cultivation in common. But no national reasons as yet compelled a change. Agriculture was still unprogressive. No large demands for food arose from growing towns. If the open-field system did little more than feed the producers, it maintained a considerable population on the land ; it gave them an interest in its management and a livelihood which was independent of any masters but themselves. During the next hundred years all this was changed. England suddenly passed from a leisurely agricultural country into a hustling industrial nation. Huge populations, gathered round centres of trade and manufacture, cried aloud for bread and meat. As the century neared its close, the demand grew more urgent under the pressure of a great war and fear of famine. Meanwhile, new agricultural resources had accumulated. The nation had the means of doubling, or even trebling, its home-grown supply of food ; but on the open-field system they could not be adopted. As long as the arable land was from harvest to seed time a common pasture, and as long as the village flocks and herds grazed the triennial fallows it was impossible to introduce roots and grasses into field cultivation.

National necessity demanded drastic change in

The Hitch Field

the old village farms. At East Hendred some effort was made to utilize the grasses which their neighbour Jethro Tull, the greatest natural genius whom English farming has produced, had done so much to introduce. On his farm at Mount Prosperous, in the village of Shalbourn—some twelve miles distant across the Downs—he had, for thirty years, 1709-40, drilled turnips and grown clover and sanfoin. Ocular demonstration may have convinced some partner in the village farm who, with his own eyes, had seen the crops in the fields. In 1767, regulations framed by the partner show that they had agreed to exclude their stock from the "Hitch Field," in which they grew clover and sanfoin. Neither artificial grasses nor roots were, however, introduced into the medieval rotation of winter or spring corn, followed by a fallow, under which the bulk of the arable land was cropped. The Hitch Field was a palliative, not a remedy, for the waste of the productive powers of the soil.

The end was not long deferred. In 1800 Sir John Pollen, Basil Eyston, and Richard Hopkins, "Esquires," three other landowners described as "gentlemen," ten yeomen, a blacksmith, a cordwainer, and a mason petitioned Parliament for an Enclosure Act. It was passed in 1801, and three Commissioners were appointed "to divide, allot and lay in severalty the open and common fields, common meadows, common pastures, Downs and other commonable and waste lands in that part of the Parish of East Hendred which lies in the Westmanside Hundred of Wantage." The Commissioners met for the first time in June, 1801, and before the end of the year their award was issued. Notices were given in the Press and on the church door of each stage in the proceedings. Claims were considered at two special meetings. To pay expenses, seventy-eight acres, two thirds of which were Down lands, were sold by auction. Compensation was awarded to four Lords of Manors for their rights and interests in the soil of the commons and wastes lying within their respective boundaries. The total area so allotted is nine acres, the King receiving the largest allotment (three acres, three roods, thirty-two poles) in respect of the King's Manor. The award then distributed the 1,250 acres of the village farm in compact blocks among thirty-six persons, of whom the Rector was one. A few years later, the rest of the parish was similarly enclosed.

The story of the enclosure of East Hendred is that of hundreds of other villages. During the reign of George III., the modern division of the rural population became so uniform that the existence of the older system was in a few years forgotten. The intermediate links in the social scale, once so finely graduated that, at the points of transition, the divisions were scarcely perceptible, have dropped out. Capital and labour, employers and employed, confront each other with all the buffers gone. Where corn-growing continued, improved methods created a brisk demand for labour. Population rather rose than fell. At East Hendred, for instance, the number grew from 683 in 1801 to 949 in 1851; since that date, they declined, till in 1911 they had fallen to 728. Economically, the change of system was justified by success. After the country had recovered from its collapse at the close of the French War, agriculture entered on a period of solid prosperity greater than it enjoyed before or since. Popular gibes at the new standard of living among farmers are illustrated by some

Effect of Enclosures

lines from the manuscript farm-book of John Robey, a yeoman of East Hendred :

1743	1843
Man, to the Plough.	Man, Tally Ho !
Wife, to the Cow.	Miss, Piano.
Girl, to the Yarn.	Wife, Silk and Satin.
Boy, to the Barn.	Boy, Greek and Latin.
And your Rent will be netted.	And you'll all be Gazetted.

On the displaced village farmers the effects were less favourable. The compact holdings which they were allotted may have corresponded in money value with the land and rights that they had lost ; but they were generally small. Many sold their lots at the high prices which land commanded during the Napoleonic War. With the capital, some became tenant farmers, some started business in towns. Others spent the money, fell into the ranks of landless labour and, as weekly wage-earners, cultivated the soil which they and their ancestors had tilled as co-partners. With the break-up of the village farm, community life shrivelled at the core. One by one common interests and corporate activities died out. With them, accelerated by access to towns, departed the variety of occupation. Everywhere, villages were brought into touch with the outside world by improved roads and facilities of transport. At East Hendred, for instance, at five o'clock every Sunday evening, a six-horse wagon had left the village for London. A few years later, a stage-coach ran three times a week to London from Wantage, and another from the neighbouring village of Blewbury ; but the seats were few and the charges high. Now, several times a day, a motor-bus, plying between Wantage and Abingdon and Oxford, passes almost at the doors of the village.

Country Villages

It is to the good that the outlook is widened. Otherwise the change has not been entirely advantageous. In most villages it has helped to destroy small trades and industries, and so to intensify the monotony of occupation which already characterizes rural life. Local and domestic industries, on which the older self-supporting organization depended for its existence, have been swept into the towns. The clock cannot be put back, and some have gone for ever. Everywhere, spinning-wheels and weaving-looms have long been silenced. Brewing, tanning, milling are taking flight. Even baking is a lost art in the cottage. Small trades are passing away. Carriers cease to ply; tailors and cobblers put up their shutters. Businesses which are adjuncts of agriculture are failing; saddlers and wheelwrights are closing their shops; carpenters and blacksmiths are, in many cases, barely holding on. The " last man " in the village promises to be the farm-worker or the publican. Even the farm-worker's position is insecure. Without any subsidiary employments for bad times or slack seasons, he has become entirely dependent on the purchasing power of his agricultural earnings. If the land cannot pay his wages, he has no alternative resource.

Alone among European countries, England attempts to charge the land with the exclusive support of agricultural workers. The failure of this comparatively new policy is evident in the decay of villages and the congestion of towns. If agriculturalists have connived at it in order to secure the dependence of labourers, they may have cause to regret their want of foresight. Foreign nations pursue the opposite course. Take, for instance, France and Germany. France has never let go of her rural industries. Apart from her peasant proprietors, she employs some three million agricultural workers. Of these, 600,000 resemble our own men in being landless earners of weekly wages by farm-work. But there is this important difference. The great bulk of them also have subsidiary remunerative employments in rural industries. They are not troubled by winter slackness on the farm, nor is the industry hampered by the overhead charge of paying wages at a season when they cannot be earned. More valuable to us is the experience of Germany, because the amazing prosperity—I speak only of pre-war conditions —of her minor industries is the fruit of recent and deliberate policy. Founded on a Report on economic conditions in 1875, a special Department was set up in 1882 to promote the industrial development of rural districts, to level up conditions as between town and country, and to foster the progress of intensive farming. In all three objects success has been remarkable. Numerous whole-time and half-time employments, many of which are seasonally supplementary to farm-work, have been revived or created on economic yet profitable lines.

The experience may be useful. Without increasing means of occupation and of livelihood, nothing can revive English villages. " Rural industries " inadequately express employments which are only rural because they are carried on in the country, and the expression has a bad name. Nevertheless the subject has an important bearing on two urgent problems—unemployment and agricultural depression. A third may be added. It is through their minor industries, carried on in wholesome conditions, that France and Germany have absorbed their disabled soldiers. It is because we have nothing similar that we have relatively failed.

One point may be added. Under the Development Commission, a small organization has been for four years at work. It consists of two branches working closely together. One is an intelligence branch, exploring the economic possibilities of industrial development in country districts, including all handicrafts and domestic industries, whether new or old, and whether mechanical processes are used or not. The other is a co-operative trading association for the purpose of placing orders, disposing of produce, supplying material, and other similar objects. They have proceeded with the greatest caution, and on a small scale. But, whatever may be the future of land, their work will not be wasted.

At present prices, neither agricultural workers nor small-holders can neglect the supplementary employments and " domestic budgets " by which other countries retain their rural populations on the land.

CHAPTER VI

THE FOOD CAMPAIGN, 1916-18

ENCLOSURES released the energies of farmers from the medieval restrictions of village farms. On the principle of scope for individual enterprise, agriculture was reorganized and made triumphant progress. Nineteenth-century farmers learned to value their independence and prize their freedom. Yet during the last two years of the Great War they accepted the sacrifice of both. They submitted to State control; they co-operated with the Government in the effort to increase production: in spite of harassing difficulties, they raised more human food than had been produced from the land during the previous forty years. Fear of compulsion had its influence. But, in the main, the incentive of increased production was patriotism, though it may have graded downwards from the highest form to the selfish desire to save their skins from the consequences of defeat. It is the presence of this overmastering motive which prevents the period from affording any reliable precedent for the success of State control without the stimulus given by the war.

The Food Campaign of 1916-18 is already ancient history. Its causes and results, its successes and failures, are almost forgotten. Yet, from two points of view, it has an interest for the present and the future. If ever a similar emergency arose, it would serve as both a guide and a warning. The control which, in the last stages of the war, the State exercised over industries, has also profoundly influenced the trend of contemporary politics. It has stimulated the growth of Socialism. Of this control of industry by the State agriculture was an example, and it is significant that the Land Policy of the Independent Labour Party closely follows, and, in all its main details, adopts, the organization created in the course of the Food Campaign. For these reasons, it is desirable that the story should be authoritatively told by the Minister who was charged by the Government with the task of stimulating the production of home-grown food during the last stages of the Great War of 1914-18.

For convenience the material is divided into four sections.

SECTION I

ORGANIZATION OF THE INDUSTRY

The war was fought on a colossal scale. It was a death-grapple not merely of nations, but of groups of nations. As the struggle swayed backwards and forwards, the danger-spot continually shifted. Now men, now munitions, now money, now tonnage, became the most pressing need for the moment. But, during the last two years of the conflict, the question of food daily increased in urgency. The war threatened to turn on endurance. Final victory might well rest with the nation which could command the last sack of wheat or the last hundredweight of meat. In such circumstances, national necessities inevitably overruled agricultural expediencies at every turn. To meet those varying necessities as they successively arose, an elaborate organization of the farming industry was established.

The months of November and December, 1916, had been marked by a serious increase in the submarine menace. It was a foretaste of worse to come. On January 31, in the following year, the German Government presented a note to the United States Ambassador at Berlin that from February 1 it proposed to abandon all restrictions on the use of its fighting weapons at sea. Thus Germany entered on her unlimited U-boat campaign, designed to destroy the transport facilities of the Allies and cut off all sea-borne supplies from Great Britain, France and Italy. The blow was well informed, and well timed. It caught us after a poor harvest. At the end of March, 1917, our stocks of wheat and flour were low. We were faced with a serious shortage of potatoes. Our purchases of wheat in Australia were inaccessible. In America, though fortunately she had a big carry-over from the phenomenal crop of 1915, the harvest of 1916 had fallen considerably below the average of late years. Two and a half years of war, the drain on manpower, and the loss of territory were telling severely on the resources of our Allies. France and Italy showed ominous signs of a decreased capacity for production. Both in Great Britain and in the United

The Food Campaign, 1916-18

States the area of winter-sown wheat was known to be reduced. No substantial addition to our home-grown supplies of bread-stuffs could be expected before September, 1918. Moreover, Germany was convinced that British agriculture, for several years before the war, had become so depressed and enfeebled that it was incapable of any serious effort to increase production. She had, therefore, high hopes of the success of her submarine campaign. To give it time to take effect was one of the motives which led her, in the early part of 1917, to retire to a depth of thirty miles on a hundred miles of the Western Front. So confident was she of its speedy result that, in order to carry it out completely, she was ready to risk the hostility of America. On her estimate of time, the United States could not intervene effectively in the war till the world-tonnage had been so reduced as to make it impossible for the Allies to continue the struggle.

During the first few months of 1917, the campaign succeeded on so startling a scale that Germany might well be hopeful of its final triumph. The rate of destruction of ocean-going tonnage more than trebled ; it reached its highest point in March and April, 1917. In the last fortnight of the latter month, seventy-three ocean-going British ships were destroyed, as compared with a monthly average of twenty-four in 1916. On that scale of destruction, an outward-bound ship had only a three to one chance of returning safely with her cargo. In the three months, April, May, June, 1917, the British Empire lost tonnage to the amount of 1,270,513 gross tons in all classes of vessels, a figure which exceeded its total loss in the whole of the previous year.

In December, 1916, even without the opening of the unlimited submarine campaign, it had become absolutely necessary to take stock of the food situation. Our Navy and Merchant Service might or might not be able to overcome the new danger. German science might strengthen the attack: British nautical skill and inventiveness might counter it successfully. No one could predict with absolute certainty whether the attack or the defence would triumph. In any case, a further reduction in our limited tonnage and a more drastic restriction of our sea-borne supplies were inevitable. The strain on the carrying capacity of shipping was already intensely severe. When America came into the war, the pressure became still more extreme. The war was certain to be prolonged, and food-production in Great Britain—still more among our Allies—showed alarming symptoms of decline. In these circumstances, the Government decided that a vigorous effort must at once be made to maintain and, if possible, increase the supplies of home-grown food in the United Kingdom.

In England the outlook was unfavourable. A poor corn-harvest, a bad potato-crop, an adverse season for autumn ploughing and sowing, a severe and, as it proved, protracted winter, were not calculated to raise the spirits of farmers. They were disheartened by the loss of labour, and discouraged by the uncertainty whether they would be able to retain any men of military age. Out of the rural population permanently employed on the land in England and Wales, some 250,000 had been already recruited for the Army. Others had left, and were daily leaving, the farms for work in munition factories, camp-building or other national occupations. Skilled ploughmen were already scarce. Half the steam tackle sets were out of action, either from loss of drivers or from defective parts. Repairs of all kinds were difficult of execution. Blacksmiths, wheelwrights, saddlers, harness-makers were serving in such numbers that wide districts were almost denuded of these indispensable industries. In October, 1917, inquiry showed that, in twenty-six administrative counties, the shops of 515 blacksmiths and 216 wheelwrights were closed, and that those of 706 blacksmiths and 428 wheelwrights were under-staffed. Some of the farm horses were unshod; others had been commandeered. Threshing machines had been taken over for military purposes. The staffs of seed-firms were depleted. Manufacturers of implements, agricultural machinery and fertilizers were employed in making munitions of war. The very first cut into imported produce which was necessitated by the loss of tonnage reduced the normal imports of raw fruits and vegetables by 52,000 tons a month, and of food-stuffs for man and beast at a monthly rate of 77,000 tons. It also restricted the import of the ingredients of fertilizers, such as phosphatic rock (North Africa) and iron pyrites (Spain). The immense demand for munitions of war told heavily on the available supply of sulphate of ammonia and sulphuric acid. Manufacturers of superphosphates who had sulphuric acid had no phosphatic rock and *vice versâ*. Potash from the German sources of Stassfurt had disappeared from our markets with the declaration of war; the attempt to obtain supplies from Abyssinia failed. Shipping was not available for the transport of Chilian nitrates. As soon as the export trade in basic slag was stopped, much larger quantities were available for home consumption; but we were short of grinding machines, and of the men to work them. Lime-kilns were closed, because the lime-burners were at the front.

A Hearing for Agriculture

All these requisites, from labour to fertilizers, were necessities of arable cultivation. Without them it seemed impossible that the area under the plough could be maintained ; still less could it be reasonably expected to expand. At the same time, ordinary methods of transacting business were interrupted ; normal channels of supply were blocked ; internal transport facilities were strictly curtailed ; agriculture was in a great degree powerless to help itself ; farmers as individuals seemed too crippled to make an extra effort.

Agriculture was the last industry to receive official aid. It found what might be considered to be its territory already occupied by great Departments of State, strongly backed by public opinion, and powerfully organized to discharge duties which might conflict with the claims of the latest comer. Reinforcements were urgently needed for the Army : but to the land labour was equally essential. High prices would stimulate the production of food ; but in the interests of consumers the cost of necessaries had to be strictly controlled. Imported food-stuffs and fertilizers might be vital to the meat supply and to arable cultivation ; but the first call on tonnage lay with the military authorities and the Ministry of Munitions. Without soldiers and munitions the war could not be ended ; without food it could not be prolonged. Before agriculture could obtain a hearing, it had not only to arouse farming opinion, but to make the urgency of its needs felt by the Press, by politicians and by the people. Without the warm sympathy and courageous optimism of the Prime Minister, the task could not have been accomplished.

Memory is short-lived. But no one who has before him the documentary evidence of the day will say that the foregoing picture is darkened with exaggerated gloom. In the winter of 1916-17, the cry of " Back to the Seventies " sounded like the words of an idle dreamer, talking in his sleep. Yet, eighteen months later, the dream seemed likely to become an accomplished fact. A corn harvest, which promised to equal that of 1868, was actually in sight. It was not all gain. On this point more will be said later. Two wet months damaged the crop in the North of England. But, even when the losses of that disastrous September and October and the displacement of pasture had been liberally discounted, the net results were considerable. They showed, according to the official calculation, that, as compared with the average of the peace years 1904-13, the farmers of England and Wales had added to the home-grown output of human food a quantity equivalent to a saving of 2,300,000 tons of shipping space. Adopting the estimate that 5,000 tons of cargo are equivalent to 1,000 soldiers and their equipment, farmers had set free sufficient tonnage to bring to Europe nearly half a million soldiers from the United States.

The campaign for increased food production opened with a speech from the President of the Board of Agriculture on December 20, 1916, at a meeting in London of the Federation of War Agricultural Committees, with Sir Mark Collet in the chair. It was followed up by two circular letters from the Board of December 28 and 29. The Board proceeded on the lines of the recommendations contained in the Interim Report of the Milner Committee, July 17, 1915, of which the President had been a member. It recognized from the first that the willing co-operation of farmers in the movement was essential to success, and that, without agricultural opinion behind the effort, it was foredoomed to failure. Apart from general policy, there must be no farming from Whitehall. On the other hand, the Board knew that the need was urgent, and that it might prove necessary to force its plans on a reluctant minority of farmers. Thus, the three main features of the movement were the improvement and extension of arable cultivation, with spade as well as plough ; decentralization ; and drastic powers of compulsion which could only be justifiable or tolerable in a war emergency.

The plough policy was admittedly dictated by the Board. But, in its general principles, it was imposed on the agricultural industry by national necessities. The interruption of sea-borne trade and the strain upon the reduced tonnage threatened our supplies of food from three special directions. Our imports of grain, of concentrated cattle-food, and of artificial fertilizers were in jeopardy. The three danger-spots were, therefore, bread-stuffs for human food, winter milk and winter meat, and the maintenance or restoration of the fertility of exhausted arable land. Increased output might be obtained by grading up the average cultivation of the existing arable acreage, and by the utilization of derelict land. But no results commensurate with national needs could be expected from these sources only. To meet the large war demands for increased corn and winter fodder, the existing area under the plough was inadequate, and it was impossible to " keep off the grass," because the release of its stored-up fertility dispensed with the need of imported fertilizers.

The problem was that of providing for the subsistence of the nation. Given the circumstances, it is difficult to suggest any other policy than the extension of the arable acreage. Every farmer is aware

The Food Campaign, 1916-18

that tillage more than trebles the output of human food. In 1870 the land fed 26 million people. In 1914 it fed 16 millions. The reason for the decline was the restricted area under the plough. Summer milk and summer meat off grass were never in serious danger ; the highest demand made by the ploughing programmes of 1917-18 did not exceed one-eighth of the existing area of permanent grass. According to the Board's calculation, there was meat in sight for at least two years and a sufficient, if reduced, yield of milk.

The general policy then was to secure the adequate cultivation and cropping of arable land, and to extend its area by ploughing up suitable grass. It could only be carried out by decentralization. Several hundreds of thousands of separate businesses could not be treated, like factories, as controlled establishments. Local farmers were the best judges, in their own districts, of insufficient cultivation, and of the most suitable land to be brought under the plough. An organization already existed which might be adapted and utilized for the purpose. On the recommendation of the Milner Committee of 1915, War Agricultural Committees had been set up in most of the Counties. Where they existed, their activity and efficiency varied greatly. In almost all cases, they were unwieldy bodies for any purposes except those of consultation and advice. To carry out the new policy, small executive committees were necessary. They were formed by asking the War Agricultural Committees to appoint not more than seven members, who, together with such additional appointments as the Board might make, constituted the County Agricultural Executive Committees. These smaller bodies, established in each County or County Division, became the local agents of the

Board. To them were delegated many of the powers which it exercised under the Defence of the Realm Regulations, and those which were afterwards retained in the Corn Production Act of 1917.

In the final shape of the local organization, the County Executives were assisted by District Committees, and, in some cases, by Parish Representatives. Each of the sixty-one Executives was provided with the necessary funds for staff and office expenses, and, as their work developed, they formed Sub-Committees for such branches as Survey, Cultivation, Supplies, Labour, Machinery, Horticulture, and Finance. During 1918 they were also entrusted with the responsibility of supplying recruits for the Army, and with protecting agriculturists who were not to be called up for military service. Their discharge of these delicate duties was warmly commended by the recruiting authorities. The members of the Executive Committees, the majority of whom were farmers actively engaged in business, gave their time, knowledge and experience without pay or reward. They brought to their work a judgment and a patriotic energy that were beyond all praise. Their most difficult and invidious task was performed with a tact and fairness which reduced the inevitable friction to a minimum.

Finally, the Counties were grouped into twenty-one districts, to each of which a District Commissioner was appointed by the Board. An *ex-officio* member of the County Executive Committees in his district, he served as a link between the Committees and headquarters. Acting under the District Commissioners were thirty-six Sub-Commissioners, whose special duties were to superintend the work of District Committees. By means of this network of local organization, each parish was, as it were, connected with the Food Production Department, which represented the Board at Whitehall.

The powers of control were extremely drastic and far-reaching. The first Cultivation of Lands Order, which vested in the Executive Committees many of the powers of the Board, was sealed on January 18, 1917. It was at once circulated to the Committees, with explanatory instructions for their guidance in its administration. The primary object which the Committees were directed to keep before them was to see that farmers were assisted and encouraged to cultivate their existing arable land, so as to secure the greatest possible output of essential food. Where grass-land could be more profitably used in the national interest as arable, they were empowered to require it to be broken up, or to break it up themselves. Schemes for the cultivation of derelict or waste land were only to be undertaken when the Committees were satisfied that the labour and machinery at their disposal could not be more advantageously applied to the land already under cultivation. The Committees were empowered to serve notices upon an occupier, requiring him to cultivate his land as they might direct in the interest of increased food production, or specifying the grass fields to be broken up. In order to secure prompt action, no appeal was allowed. Failure to comply with notices rendered the occupier liable to fine or imprisonment. Committees were further empowered to take possession of the whole or part of a farm, and either cultivate it themselves, or let it to a new tenant. The Board retained in its own hands the power to determine, or authorize an owner to determine, forthwith the tenancy of a badly cultivated farm.

It was too late in the farming season to attempt

any considerable addition to arable land for the harvest of 1917. But Committees were asked to make a rapid survey of their districts in order to report what might be done in the spring. For the harvest of 1918 they were requested to make a more detailed and careful survey. They were also promised that, in the early summer, *quota* of the additional area of food crops should be furnished, showing the arable acreage which the Government aimed at securing in each County. By the end of January, 1917, most of the Executive Committees were established. Some had already made good progress with the preliminary survey, and were taking steps to stimulate cultivation. In these preliminary surveys valuable and unpaid assistance was given by large numbers of professional men.

Other steps were taken to complete the skeleton of the necessary organization. The Board itself was not equipped to help the industry to increase production. In the past, its range of duties had been relatively restricted. To meet the new needs, the Food Production Department was constituted January 1, 1917, as a new branch of the Board, with the novel functions of distributing labour, machinery and supplies of feeding stuffs, fertilizers and other requisites, and of making arrangements necessary to help farmers to cultivate their land to the best advantage. The Department was at first under the direction of Mr. (now Sir Thomas) Middleton. After February 19, 1917, it was placed in the charge of Sir Arthur (now Viscount) Lee. Magnificently organized, it became the pivot of the whole movement. Its services to the agricultural industry were immense and many-sided. The whole was under the direction of Lord Lee. From the first he recognized the magnitude and complexity of the task. By his organizing power he perfected the machine, and by his vigour and energy made it a live force, full of enthusiasm and self-devotion.

The Department worked in seven Divisions. Local organization was in the hands of Mr. (now Sir Francis) Floud ; the Technical Division was under Sir Thomas Middleton, Labour under Lord Goschen, Women under Miss (now Dame) Meriel Talbot, Cultivation under Sir Sothern Holland, Supplies under Mr. (now Sir Lawrence) Weaver, Horticulture, including allotments, under Professor (now Sir Frederick) Keeble. Through this Department the needs of the industry were, as far as possible, met, and difficult and often protracted negotiations with other Ministries were conducted. Not the least of the difficulties was that of the accommodation of the staff. No single building being available, the work was distributed in thirteen separate premises at a considerable distance from one another. The President, besides being in daily touch with the Director-General, took the chair at weekly conferences with the heads of divisions and branches, and was responsible for the actions of the Department to the Cabinet and to Parliament.

For all scientific questions bearing on food production, a highly skilled staff of technical experts, drawn from Research Institutes and Agricultural Colleges, was formed at the end of January, 1917, with Mr. F. D. Acland as Chairman. To this Committee were referred the numerous points requiring scientific investigation which arose in the course of the campaign. Finally, for the personal assistance of the President in practical questions, and in the bearing of Schemes and Orders on farm work in different parts of the country, an Advisory Committee was established. It met fortnightly for the first eighteen months of the campaign, and rendered invaluable and unpaid help. The farming members of the President's Committee were Sir Walter Berry (Kent), and Messrs. S. W. Farmer (Wilts), Samuel Kidner (Somerset), A. Moscrop (Yorkshire), H. Padwick (Sussex), R. G. Patterson (Staffordshire), George Rea (Northumberland), Professor W. Somerville, and the Hon. Edward Strutt (Essex).

The position of transport and of food supplies compelled the Board to make light of difficulties. In many respects, history was repeating itself. With contrasts as well as parallels, the situation of 1801-15 was reproduced. To our ancestors, struggling in the throes of the Napoleonic War, a paramount consideration was the provision of bread. Whatever could be done to bring in corn from abroad, was done. The results were meagre. From 1801 to 1815 we only succeeded in obtaining an annual average supply of 600,000 quarters of wheat, sufficient for the maintenance of little more than 150,000 families. The bread of fourteen millions of people in 1801, and in 1815 of eighteen millions, depended on the weather and the efforts of agriculturists at home. In spite of an exceptional series of indifferent harvests, the prodigious efforts of farmers averted actual famine, and even, in the one favourable season (1813), produced a surplus which was carried over to the two following years. To a partial extent the position seemed likely to be repeated in 1917 and 1918. At both periods, the way of safety lay in increased production on a larger arable acreage.

In several respects, the problem was simpler during the French War than during the recent conflict. Our ancestors were better off for agricultural labour; the land was never so depleted of skilled workers as it was in the later struggle. At both periods, it was necessary to save, as well as to grow, more food, and similar measures were taken to enforce economy. But in 1801 public opinion was ready-made to help. In 1917 it had to be instructed and created. It was not only that the standard of living had been raised, and that the country might well have revolted against hardships to which our ancestors were bred and inured. At the time of the French wars, men, women and children knew from experience the need of " eating within their tether," as well as their dependence on the weather for a scarcity or sufficiency of bread. In the German war, a generation had grown up, which had never realized the importance of home-grown food, and could not conceive the possibility of their exclusion from foreign markets, in one or more of which the harvests had been abundant.

Still more striking is a difference, which illustrates the profound change of social and political conditions and thought in the twentieth century. It is the care that, in the recent war, was taken of consumers. Our ancestors attempted neither rationing nor regulation of prices. They relied on the high cost of food to enforce economy and stimulate production. There was no restriction of producers' profits in the interests of consumers. The incentive of high gains spurred agriculturists to gigantic efforts. But, in the German war, the appeal was rather to the patriotism than to the pockets of farmers. In the interests of consumers flat maximum prices were fixed for agricultural produce; the 4-lb. loaf was stabilized at 9d., partly at the expense of farmers whose home-grown wheat was taken at lower prices than were paid to foreign producers ; the best and worst qualities of home-grown meat were sold at the same price, in order that the long and the short purses might in this respect be on an equality. That the principle on which prices were thus regulated was wise, will not be disputed. But it did not make the problem of increasing production more easy of solution. One of the sharpest spurs to exertion was blunted.

It is enough to indicate generally the interesting parallels and contrasts between England's position in the French and in the German wars. Other points of resemblance or of difference will probably suggest themselves in the detailed story of the recent movement to increase supplies of home-grown food.

In the months of January and February, 1917, numerous meetings were held in different parts of the country, at which the Board's plan was explained to farmers by the President. It met with as good a reception as could be expected. The plough policy imposed some real sacrifices upon both landowners and farmers. The fact was frankly recognized. It was not a question whether a better or an easier livelihood was to be made from feeding stock on grass or from the crops grown on arable land. The only question was by which method of husbandry the largest number of mouths could be fed—and to that there was but one answer. But the agricultural community did not, and indeed could not, at first realize the full gravity of the situation. In effect they said : "Give us the men and the fertilizers, and we will raise the food." On those terms they were willing and eager to do their utmost. But those were exactly the conditions which could not be satisfied.

The Food Campaign, 1916-18

In many directions farmers saw practical difficulties. Above all, they felt three uncertainties which sapped their confidence. The first was the fear of losing the scanty labour still on the land. The calling up in January, 1917, of 30,000 agricultural workers seemed to threaten worse things to come. There had been no method in the early stages of volunteering or recruiting. In some cases farms had been stripped of their skilled labour, and the call had told more heavily on some counties than on others. The feeling was strongly and almost universally expressed that, unless the labour situation was improved, production could not even be maintained at its present level. The second was the fear of the action of the Food Controller in fixing agricultural prices. From the nature of his duties farmers were suspicious that he would necessarily incline to favour consumers at the expense of producers. The third was the dread of a rapid fall of prices at the close of the war. To be caught, when the slump came, with a large arable area might spell ruin. Thousands realized the risk from actual experience of the past ; to all, it was the nightmare of the future.

Farmers knew that they could double their output, if they were enabled to work on the same conditions as Munition Factories, with unlimited labour, with unrestricted prices for their produce, with abundant supplies of the raw materials of their industry, with every form of priority, and with protection for their men. But, for anything like this favourable position, agriculture was two years too late. The nation was now too far advanced towards exhaustion in man-power, tonnage and finance—apart from the danger of leaving the market for necessaries of life uncontrolled—

to allow the remotest approach to those conditions. The task that farmers were asked to undertake was totally different. Agricultural workers who had become efficient soldiers could not be permanently released from the front. Even the skilled labour still retained on farms remained there subject to the uncertainties of the paramount requirements of military service. Farmers' prices must be controlled in the interests of consumers. Their demands on the carrying capacity of our shipping for feeding-stuffs or fertilizers must rank behind the transport of men and material for military exigencies. The only security which could be given was that, if they grew wheat or oats after the passing of the Corn Production Act of 1917, the nation would guarantee them, not profits, but safety from substantial loss. It was admittedly cold encouragement, though it did protect farmers from the devastating break in prices which had ruined thousands in the previous century. With justice they complained that in the " nineties " the nation had eaten its cheap food without bestowing a thought on the widespread ruin which it brought on the agricultural community ; but, as soon as the fiscal system told in favour of home producers, it clamoured for control of prices.

It was, however, increasingly evident that, in the interest of British agriculture, the threatened decline in food production must be arrested. Were it allowed to continue, agriculture would not be worth considering ; it would sink into the class of non-essential industries, and its man-power would be treated as a reserve on which the Army would draw at will with the full approval of the nation. If the output of food decreased, the men were of more immediate use in the camp than on

The Food Campaign, 1916-18

the land. But, if the farming industry pulled its weight in the national effort, if farmers could turn the threatened decline into a great advance, relieve tonnage and increase food supplies, public opinion might be enlisted in their support. In the one direction lay the complete ruin of the industry ; in the other, its modified prosperity.

As has already been stated, farmers daily became more powerless as individuals to help themselves, or to carry on their business on the old independent lines. Neither the Board nor its newly created Food Production Department was ever in a position to make unconditional promises of help in respect of such agricultural requisites as labour, machinery, feeding stuffs and fertilizers, petrol and paraffin. All these necessities were already controlled by other Departments in other national interests. Thus, the War Office had the last word in the supply of all forms of military labour and of German prisoners. Interned aliens depended on the Home Office. Civilian labour was controlled by the Minister of National Service. The supply of machinery and implements, home-made or imported, rested with the Ministry of Munitions, on whom the Board indented for its needs. The supply of petrol and paraffin was in the hands of the Petrol Committee. Feeding-stuffs were under the control of the Ministry of Food. Fertilizers belonged, at first, to the Ministry of Food, afterwards to the Ministry of Munitions, though in practice the actual distribution of the home-produced supply was ultimately controlled by the Supplies Division of the Food Production Department on behalf of the Board. The prices of wool, it may be added, as well as those of hay and straw, for military use were regulated by the War Office. Apart from the rapid fluctuations in the overruling exigencies of national needs, it is obvious from the enumeration of controlling bodies that the Board was never able to give to farmers those absolute assurances of supply that they not unreasonably demanded.

The great difficulty, which stared the campaign in the face wherever it turned, was the regulation of prices. Every article of food was regulated by the Food Controller, subject only to formal and perfunctory consultation with the President of the Board of Agriculture. No one had had any previous experience of the difficulties of fixing prices. No useful sets of figures were available for estimating costs of production. In normal times, varying rates, determined by the play of local markets, make the necessary adjustment between district and district. Now, flat rates had to be fixed, and what was one farmer's meat was another's poison. One man might get too much, another too little. Everyone knows, for example, that the cost of producing a quarter of wheat differs not only in each county, but on nearly every farm, and on nearly every field. The outstanding question which persistently recurred was, how far prices should be regulated to stimulate production or in the interests of consumption. The nation wanted all the food it could get ; but farmers could only produce as much as they could afford. One Food Controller might say : " Produce the stuff and I will see you paid." His successor might say : " Consumers can only pay so much, and that must be the producer's price."

Agriculturists strongly urged that the President of the Board of Agriculture should also hold the office of Food Controller. That was the system adopted in France. But no comparison between

The Food Campaign, 1916-18

the two countries is possible.   In France, one-half
of the population are producers, and the Minister
administers agriculture for the whole country.   In
the United Kingdom, the President of the English
Board of Agriculture had little control in Scotland
and none at all in Ireland.   It must be admitted
that the complete separation of the two offices
led to misunderstandings on the part of the agricultural community which impaired the influence
of the Board.   Heart-burning is inseparable from
price-fixing.   It was annoying and sometimes unintelligible to farmers to find prices cut down of
all that they had to sell : it was still more irritating
to find prices rising of all that they had to buy.
At a later stage, the Government subsidy on bread
became a burning question.   The price paid for
wheat to home-producers was sometimes less by
two-fifths than that paid for foreign bread-stuffs.
Every quarter grown at home reduced the expenditure abroad, and the burden of the taxpayer was
relieved, at the expense of the British farmer, by
an aggregate sum which in the years 1917-20 was
certainly not less than £20,000,000.

At the same time the prices for home-grown corn
and their relation to prices of other agricultural
produce were discouraging to the plough policy.
Farmers were able to make much larger profits on
meat and milk produced on grass than they could
obtain from corn grown on arable land.   On the
other hand, it may be very strongly urged that
consumers would not have tolerated the regulation
of prices by the representative of producers and that
farmers obtained from the Food Controller a higher
general range of prices than the public would have
accepted if they had been fixed by the Board of
Agriculture alone.   Yet, in theory, and occasionally,

perhaps, in practice, farmers suffered. What was still more unfortunate was that they fancied themselves unfairly treated. It was obvious that a Food Controller, with nine-tenths of the public behind him, could afford to ignore the claims, however persistently they might be urged, of the official representative of the remaining tenth ; the louder producers squealed, the louder consumers applauded.

Another difficulty which threatened the campaign was the apathy of public opinion. For years the national importance of agriculture at home had been ignored. The lost ground had to be recovered. With all the facts and figures constantly before them, it was easy for the Government to realize the necessity of increasing the production of home-grown food. Without the fullest information, it was harder to convince public and farming opinion of the gravity of the situation. The Press gave most valuable help. But general statements, however ably made, do not arrest attention. It is the definite facts that carry conviction. A chart, posted in every town and village, showing from day to day the fluctuations in our stocks of food, and the gradual shrinkage in the carrying capacity of shipping, would have forced the nation to appreciate its danger. Such a course was, for many obvious reasons, so inadvisable as to be impossible. For many months, neither consumers nor producers realized the fact and the consequences of the interruption of our sea-borne supplies.

Consumers had been so long accustomed to send, as it were, round the corner, and buy from the foreigner whatever bread and meat were required, that they could not grasp the new situation. The tonnage was not there to bring home their purchases.

The Food Campaign, 1916-18

Bewildered by the novelty, they abused the British farmer, forgetting that their insistence on cheap food had elbowed him out of the market. On the other hand, producers were equally slow to realize the truth, although every safe opportunity was taken to make known telling facts. For this purpose the President's Advisory Committee was always useful. It was also possible to speak with some degree of openness at private conferences with chairmen, commissioners and officials of Executive Committees in London, or at the private meetings of the Committees themselves which preceded every public meeting in the Counties. But the process was necessarily slow. Warnings of the coming scarcity of foreign oats, barley, maize, oil seeds and cake, received little attention, or were met, even to the end of the campaign, by the question, " Why not bring them in from America ? "

In January, 1918, an unprecedented demand for meat had severely reduced the number of cattle at home which were capable of being ripened for slaughter : foreign imports of beef and mutton for civilian supply had almost entirely ceased ; our barley was needed for human food ; offals, owing to closer milling, had lost two-thirds of their feeding value ; the foreign imports on which feeders and dairymen mainly relied for winter meat and winter milk were cut down to the bone ; for the next eight months there was only sufficient concentrated food in sight to feed a reduced allowance to working horses, transport as well as farm, and cows in milk. There was nothing over for fatting cattle, sheep, lambs, pigs or poultry. The actual facts and figures of the position into which we were rapidly passing were embodied in a statement drawn up by the Board for publication, in December, 1917.

Difficulties of the Campaign

But the paper was withdrawn, because it was decided by the Government to be too alarming for the public at home, and too encouraging for our enemies abroad. It was not the least of the advantages of the rationing system of 1918 that it at last convinced most members of the community that they were indeed inhabitants of " a beleaguered city."

The chief difficulties which impeded the effort to increase food production were, in the circumstances, inevitable. They remained throughout the campaign. They are not enumerated as grievances ; they are mentioned as difficulties in the way of achievement. Never at any time did farmers command an adequate supply of skilled labour ; nor, after 1917, had they, owing to fixed prices and rising costs of production, the stimulus of high profits on the staple products of their industry. Never at any time had the Board a deciding voice in fixing prices or in providing the requisites of production. For all essentials of their industry, agriculturists were dependent on Ministries whose official duties might sometimes clash with farming interests. But farmers were not the only persons who were called on to make " bricks without straw." Agriculture was but one corner of a vast field of united effort—an item in a huge reorganization of industrial and economic life for the purposes of war. In so critical a stage of the struggle, it was idle to cry for the moon. The task set to the industry, in the national interest and need, was to produce, in the shortest possible time, the largest possible quantity of the plainest and most indispensable human food. As to the means of fulfilling the task, if the ideal " bests " were impracticable, the next " bests " available must be made to do. It was in this spirit that farmers learned to tackle their difficulties.

In the attempt to increase production two periods must be distinguished. The first comprises the preparations for the harvest of 1917 ; the second those for the harvest of 1918. As will be shown later, no programme was adopted for the harvest of 1919.

SECTION II

THE HARVEST OF 1917

The eaily months of 1917 were the most trying period of the whole campaign. The labour situation, which, as time went on, gradually improved, was then at its worst. All the essential requisites of agriculture were urgently needed ; but every day revealed more clearly the complete interruption of the ordinary channels of supply. It was easy to create a paper organization capable of helping the industry in these novel conditions; time was needed to give it reality and life. The County Executive Committees had not mastered their work ; the Food Production Department was not fully manned. Naturally enough, the Board's inability to satisfy the immediate wants of farmers provoked a storm of criticism. But, on the whole, the campaign opened with the support of the Press and the goodwill of the agricultural community.

In the first weeks of the year, the courage of farmers was severely tested. Short-handed as they already were, they were urged to grow more food. Almost in the same breath they were told that their scanty supply of skilled labour must be still further cut down. At the beginning of 1917 the needs of the Army were extremely urgent. In order to take the offensive in the spring, and to co-operate efficiently with the French, larger forces, both in the field and in reserve, were essential. Recruiting had proceeded so slowly that the Army Council were unable, without heavy calls on the man-power at home, to make good their promises to our Commander-in-Chief, or to fulfil their engagements with the French. According to official estimates, there still remained on the farms in Great Britain 177,000 men of military age. From these, and similar sources in other industries, recruits had to be drawn if the spring offensive was to be undertaken. On January 16, 1917, 30,000 men, out of the 60,000 whom the War Office had claimed in the preceding October, were called up from the land. No explanation of the urgency of the military need could, of course, be given to the public. But whatever was possible was done by the War Office to ease the labour situation thus created. In exchange for the skilled sturdy men with whom they were accustomed to work, farmers were offered strangers belonging to the C III. category, unaccustomed to agricultural work, and physically unfitted for active service in the Army. These men, 11,500 in number, were formed into Agricultural Companies, and, subject to military exigencies, made available for agriculture throughout the war. At first sight the material was unpromising. Farmers grumbled that they were asked to keep infirmaries. But they responded gallantly to the appeal of the President that they should become " the Kitcheners of a new agricultural army." They were rewarded for their instruction. Many of the men improved in physique and developed unexpected capacities.

Besides these Agricultural Companies, the Army

The Food Campaign, 1916-18

Council released 12,500 men from the Home Defence Force on furlough up to April 30. Early in March the men belonging to both these classes began to arrive at the Distribution Centres, from which they were dispatched to those farmers who applied for labour through the County Executive Committees. Not more than 3,000 out of the total number of 24,000 proved to have had any experience of ploughing. On March 12, therefore, the military authorities ordered all skilled ploughmen in the United Kingdom to return to their depots on agricultural furlough up to April 30. These were the stamp of men required. By the end of the first week in April, 40,000 men of the three classes were at work on the land. Unfortunately the season was unusually late. Though the Army Council extended the furlough in all cases till May 10, 18,000 of the skilled ploughmen who belonged to category A, were recalled before the tillage was completed. Urgent requests were made for their retention. But the Army Council could not spare a single " A " man. Owing to the incomplete success of the French operations on the Aisne, our April offensive had to be renewed in May. A further attack on the Flanders front was also projected for July. In the case of the other men, the furlough was extended to July 25.

In other directions the military authorities did what they could to help the industry. They sought out, for instance, and released a considerable number of steam-tackle men for whom application was made in January, and, later on, of shepherds and shearers, though the recovery of any of the rural handicraftsmen proved more difficult. They also gave special assistance at the hay and corn harvests. The appeal of the National Service Department

Supply of Labour

for volunteers for this work proved unsuccessful. But the military authorities, though crippled by the necessity of maintaining a mobile Home Defence Force, came to the rescue. Seventeen thousand additional men began to move into the Distribution Centres in June, 1917. This portion of the story has been told in some detail, because it serves to illustrate the interdependence of the various parts of the national organization for purposes of war.

Most of the labour supplied by the military authorities was inexperienced. It was also temporary. Other sources were explored to increase the permanent staff. Old-age pensioners in rural districts, by arrangements made with the Local Government Board in January, 1917, were allowed to earn wages without forfeiting their pensions. Ultimately (April, 1918) the Treasury sanctioned their employment at weekly wages not exceeding 30s. In January, 1917, also, a scheme was agreed with the War Office for the employment of prisoners of war. But the conditions were necessarily stringent. Precautions against escape had to be taken, and arrangements made for housing, transport and commissariat. Some months were spent in preparations. By the end of July, 15 camps had been provided, employing 1,476 prisoners. In June, 1918, there were working on the land, either from 190 camps, or lodged on farms, 11,794 prisoners. The number was subsequently increased to over 30,000. Their excellent work had quickly overcome the prejudice which was at first entertained. Other schemes were arranged with the Home Office early in February, 1917, for the employment of interned aliens and of conscientious objectors. Local feeling was, however too strong against both classes. The number of aliens employed was under 2,000, and that of conscientious objectors scarcely rose above 200.

A more important source of permanent labour was found in the work of women. This side of the organization claims a chapter to itself. Here only the bare outline can be traced. An addition of 210,000 was made to the pre-war number of part-time village workers, principally owing to the public spirit of the women themselves and to the indefatigable activities of the Village Registrars and the County Committees. Living at home, familiar with rural surroundings, and available for seasonal needs, women of this class escaped the difficulty of housing, and proved especially attractive to farmers. Their labour was organized and made more efficient, and the trouble of half-time overcome, by the use of group-leaders and forewomen. In addition to the village women, a Land Army was formed of those women over eighteen years of age, who were willing to work on the land during the war, to give their whole time, and to go to any district where they were needed. An appeal for recruits was made by the President at a crowded meeting at the Albert Hall in London. A very large number of women offered themselves. But so high a standard of physical fitness was fixed that 75 per cent. were rejected. The greatest strength which the force ultimately reached was 16,000 in September, 1918. For the most part town-bred, and many of them highly educated, the Land Army was not at first acceptable to farmers. They were generally inexperienced, and there were always difficulties of housing to be faced. There was also the fear that, if women were permanently employed on the farms, the men would be taken by the War Office. This obstacle was removed in January, 1917, when the Army Council decided to treat female labour as supplementary to, and not in substitution for, male labour. Reassured on this point, farmers gave them a trial.

The quickness with which the women learnt their work, their endurance, their cheerful acceptance of hardships and discomforts conquered all difficulties. In the care of horses and live-stock, as milkers, thatchers, tractor-drivers, and even as ordinary farm-hands, they made good, and, in very adverse circumstances, did invaluable work. The Land Army deservedly became the most popular feature at any agricultural gathering. The women's contingent, both part-time and whole-time, upwards of 300,000 in number, was organized and administered by women, both at the Central Office in London and in the numerous County Committees.

One other source of temporary labour must be mentioned. As early as January, 1917, plans had been discussed for obtaining the services of public-school boys and their masters for the coming corn harvest. In the next few months, conferences were held by the Food Production Department with the National Service Department. The latter body, with the co-operation of the County Executive Committees, made excellent arrangements for the boys and their camps. Nearly 5,000 boys helped to gather in the corn harvest of 1917, and, at the corn harvest of 1918, upwards of 15,000 gave their assistance.

Numerically, the assistance given by additional workers on the land sounds imposing. It considerably exceeded 400,000 persons. But, at first, the quality of the labour of skilled and of inexperienced hands differed almost as widely as the military efficiency of an armed crowd and a disciplined army. As time went on, the improvement was very marked. But the additional burden of instruction, training and organization which was imposed on farmers was heavy. Practically, the shortage of skilled labour always remained acute. Nor did time allow either the Board or the Food Production Department to give effective aid in the approaching season of spring ploughing beyond the labour that has been mentioned. In some cases farmers were short of teams for the work. Locally, the deficiency was met by arrangements with the Army Council. Farmers in the neighbourhood of Military Camps were enabled to hire heavy draught horses, at first with, and ultimately without, their soldier drivers. A census taken of steam-tackle sets in January, 1917, and a map subsequently made of their distribution, revealed the fact that nearly half of the total number of 500 were out of action, from the want of either drivers or of repairs. Three hundred men, experienced in the work and applied for by name, were released by the military authorities, and arrangements were made to put in repair the broken-down sets. By June, 1917, all but 40 sets, which proved to be obsolete, were at work. Even for the spring ploughing something was accomplished. The Steam Cultivation Association recognized the gravity of the crisis, and agreed to the request that they would keep sets at work from daylight to dark seven days a week. By this means an increase of 25 per cent. was obtained in working hours.

It had been hoped to provide an adequate supply

of motor-tractors. The hope was frustrated by a variety of causes. The tractors could not be built in this country, because manufacturers and material were engaged in the supply of munitions. A large number were, therefore, ordered from America through the Ministry of Munitions. But the pressure on transport was so severe that few were landed in time. All the tractors that the Food Production Department could collect for the spring ploughing of 1917 consisted of 477 Government-owned machines and 135 hired from private owners, together with 54 caterpillars built for military purposes, and borrowed from the Russian Government. The use of tractors was a novelty, and was little understood. Drivers were inexperienced. Some of the machines were not of the best type ; others were employed on unsuitable land. But, even in this experimental stage, their value was so clearly established that only the most sceptical of farmers remained unconvinced. The trial was expensive, but successful. In ordinary times the introduction of tractors into field cultivation on any large scale would have taken twenty years. Under the pressure of emergency, in spite of numerous failures, it was done in three months. Prejudice was overcome by ocular demonstration, and the way paved for their extended and general use.

With such assistance in labour, horses and machinery as has been described, the spring ploughing and cropping were accomplished, and the 1917 harvest gathered. The addition to the tillage area of the United Kingdom was approximately one million acres. It was not all net gain. Against the increased corn, straw and potatoes grown on the added area must be set the loss of meat on the

The Food Campaign, 1916-18

broken-up grass. In England and Wales, for example, there were 187,420 acres of pasture ploughed, which would have added 1 cwt. of meat per acre to our food supplies. A strong point was rightly made of this loss by opponents of the plough. Their arguments were strengthened by instances of the total destruction of crops by wireworm on newly ploughed grass. In hundreds of letters the policy of the Board was denounced as that of " ignorant charlatans."

It is, of course, true that there were losses as well as gains, and that the net advantage can only be calculated by allowing for losses. But in the official estimates, the casualties were, as results showed, liberally discounted. The crops, like the men at the front, had to " go over the top." The estimated yield was put so low that a large margin of safety was allowed. Wire-worms were no new discovery. Speaking at the Farmers' Club, November 2, 1914, the President, then M.P. for the University of Oxford, had urged that, if the war was prolonged, a wheat shortage among the Allies was inevitable, and that this country might not be able to obtain its normal supplies from abroad. We might, he said, grown one-fifth more, or even three-fifths of our needs. But wheat crops on newly ploughed land were no certainty. " We all know the danger, for instance, of such creatures as the wire-worm." The risk was not therefore unknown. Nor was it forgotten. As a matter of fact, however, the successes on the newly ploughed land, judging from reports received in 1917 from 55 counties, outnumbered the failures by four to one. The usual crop was spring oats. But a great variety of other crops succeeded, such as wheat, barley, peas, beans, potatoes, mangolds, mustard. Success depended less on the choice of the crop than on the firmness of the seed-bed. Where the soil was sufficiently consolidated, the activity of the wire-worm and the effect of the drought in the early summer were checked. Much of the damage attributed to wire-worms was caused by want of proper tillage and, above all, by the absence of the roller or the land presser.

No subject opens a wider door for divergence of opinion than the conversion of pasture into tillage, and strong opposition was naturally to be expected from practical men whose livelihood was at stake. For many years of peace, live-stock farming had been paramount in the United Kingdom. It is a safe, interesting and reasonably remunerative industry, in which British farmers excel. It is less anxious than tillage, less risky and less costly, especially in labour. But in 1917 these considerations were superseded by national necessities. Quantity of food was the one supreme object. As between grass and tillage, the only question worth asking was—which of the two can support the largest number of persons ? It is answered in Sir Thomas Middleton's Table of the numbers to whom the two methods of husbandry will supply a subsistence diet for one year :—

100 acres	very poor grass	converted into meat,				2–3	persons.
,, ,,	medium ,,	,,	,,	,,	,,	12–14	,,
,, ,,	very good ,,	,,	,,	,,	,,	25–40	,,
,, ,,	mangolds (average crop)		,,	,,		35	,,
,, ,,	wheat (av.) as bread		,,	,,		200	,,
,, ,,	potatoes (av.) as vegetable		,,	,,		400	,,

From the general result of these comparative figures there is no escape. No one responsible for feeding the nation in time of war could hesitate to adopt the policy of the plough, however unpopular it might be with those whose individual interests appeared to be endangered.

The acreage actually under tillage in England and Wales in the cereal year 1916-17 showed increases in the following crops, as compared with the previous season :—

Corn (including peas)	.	.	.	.	310,769	acres.
Potatoes	.	.	.	.	80,039	,,
Turnips and swedes	.	.	.	.	34,215	,,
Mangolds	.	.	.	.	10,705	,,
					435,728	acres.

The winter sowing of wheat in 1916 had fallen by 62,617 acres ; but this decrease was made good and turned into an advance on the total acreage of the previous year by a spring sowing of 68,894 acres.

Though the intervention of the Government only became effective in the spring season of 1917, the actual weight of human food produced in the United Kingdom at the forthcoming harvest was considerably increased. Under war conditions, the three white-corn crops as well as potatoes must be treated as constituents of bread or its substitutes. Nearly six million quarters of white corn (5,827,000 quarters) were added to the production of the previous year. Measured by weight, the additional weight of wheat, barley, oats and potatoes was 3,906,000 tons. Nor can the effect of the short campaign be judged only by actual increases. The threatened decline had been arrested and turned into an advance. During the acute crisis at the close of 1917 and in the early weeks of 1918, the addition to our output of bread or its substitutes was of the utmost value. If, instead of an increase, there had been a decrease in our home-grown supplies, the

Mustard and Hops

consequences to ourselves and our Allies would have been extremely grave.

Of crop-displacements in England and Wales, those in mustard for seed, in hops and in bulbs were effected by the direct action of the Board.

In the case of mustard for seed, the demands on tonnage restricted the export trade in the manufactured article, and, in the stress of war, the land was needed for the production of human food. In 1916, 65,720 acres were under the crop, which, on suitable soils, is remunerative. Some farmers had already made their arrangements for the supply on the scale of the previous year. If action was to be taken at all, it had to be prompt. Conferences between the President and the trade resulted in an agreement to reduce the acreage by 62 per cent. The contracts for mustard seed were distributed by licences, as evenly as possible, among the districts from which the supplies are usually drawn.

Owing to the large capital invested per acre by hop-growers, the reduction of the area under hops was still more difficult. Apart from the crop itself, the cultivation, from its intensive character, is of great value to agriculture. But in the interests of producers themselves, some change was necessitated by the control of the brewing industry in 1917. In order to save tonnage, the Government decided to reduce the imports of brewing and distillery materials by 48,000 tons per month, and to cut down the barrelage of beer from the 36,000,000 barrels brewed in 1914 to an annual rate of 10,000,000 barrels, afterwards increased to about fourteen. The area of home-grown hops in 1914 was 36,661 acres; but brewing was now reduced by nearly two-thirds. If, therefore, production were maintained on the old scale, the supply would largely exceed the demand. Half the product would be unsaleable, especially as there were big stocks in hand. In the interests both of producers and of the nation, a part of the richly cultivated area could be more profitably used for the supply of human food. Conferences were held by the President and officials of the Board with hop-growers, the hop trade and the brewers, which resulted in the establishment of a Joint Committee. Imports of foreign hops were prohibited, prices regulated, and hop growers asked to reduce their acreage by slightly more than half the area which was devoted to the crops in 1916. At first, the reduction was voluntary. Subsequently, at the request of the growers themselves, it was made compulsory by an Order from the Board. On a smaller scale, a similar reduction in the area devoted to bulb-growing, and its use for human food, was carried out by the Board through arrangements with bulb-growers, especially in the Spalding district. In all cases the pecuniary sacrifice which was involved was patriotically accepted.

Among other efforts to stimulate food production may be mentioned the marked success in obtaining a larger supply of allotments, and the partial failure to increase the dwindling pig population of the country.

Under the Defence of the Realm Act, powers were delegated to Town and Urban District Councils enabling them to take possession of any unoccupied land, and with the sanction of the County Executive Committees of any occupied land, for the purpose of letting it to residents in urban areas for cultivation. In the metropolitan area similar powers were vested in the Borough Councils. In rural districts a stimulus was also given to the movement. Railway companies, colliery-owners, and private owners of land gave their help. Travelling inspectors, sent out by the horticultural division of the Food Production Department, visited local authorities to stir them to fresh efforts, and to aid them in obtaining land without incurring ruinous claims for compensation. By these and similar agencies the number of allotments was raised from the pre-war figure of 530,000 to about 1,400,000 in 1918. The enthusiasm was great. Nearly a million and a half of small producers studied the vicissitudes of the climate and the capabilities of the soil with the interest of farmers. Extraordinary successes were achieved. Crops were grown on the most unpromising material : cabbages appeared out of concrete and broccoli from brickbats. As the strain on man-power and transport grew more intense, the value of the movement became more marked. The crops were grown in the spare time of workers pursuing their daily avocations, while their wide local distribution placed food at the doors of consumers, and so relieved the carrying capacity of railways. Socially, also, the holdings were useful. They gave men a hobby, an occupation and an interest, which they could share with their wives and children.

The attempt to increase the pig population partially failed. In 1916, the number of breeding sows, as compared with the ten years' average, had fallen by 41,253, and of " other pigs " by 186,482. It was hoped that, with the increased supply of green food from the multiplication of allotments, pig-keeping might be revived as a domestic industry. In concert with the Local Government Board, a letter was sent out by the two Presidents to Urban

The Food Campaign, 1916-18

and Local Sanitary Authorities, encouraging them to relax the stringency of local by-laws. For the same object a Regulation was issued under the Defence of the Realm Act. In country districts the agency of the Rural League was used to stimulate pig-keeping. In a sporting county, people were urged by the President to "walk a pig instead of a puppy," an unfortunate phrase which aroused a storm of criticism from the surprisingly large number of persons who appeared unfamiliar with the practice to which the phrase alluded. The movement was strenuously advocated by leading agriculturists as the cheapest form of meat production. To give a further stimulus to pig-keeping, conferences were held with prominent breeders. But, as time went on, it became increasingly evident in 1918 that, owing to the acute scarcity of breadstuffs, no barley could be spared for meal. Every grain was needed for bread. Offals, owing to closer milling, were of the poorest quality. Maize was unobtainable. The Board was, therefore, obliged to alter its tactics. It had to damp down enthusiasm, and urge pig-keeping without meal.

During the summer months of 1917, Parliament was mainly occupied with the Corn Production Bill, which passed into law in August. The measure need not be discussed in detail. For a period of six years it gave the Board of Agriculture powers to enforce the plough policy and improve the cultivation of land. In return for the acceptance of control and of the increased risks of arable farming, it guaranteed growers of wheat and oats for the harvests of 1917–22 against substantial loss, if prices fell during that period. It prohibited the raising of rent where it could be shown that, without

138

The Wage Board

the guarantees, the holding could not have stood the rise. It provided machinery for fixing and enforcing minimum rates of wages for agricultural labourers. On this last-mentioned provision, a few words seem necessary.

On national and social grounds, some machinery for the regulation of rates of payment in agriculture had long been advocated. Wages south of the Trent were miserably low. But, immobile and isolated, labourers found it difficult to combine and, without combination, to enforce their demands for higher pay. Organization for the purpose of collective bargaining was inevitably a slow process, even if it eventually succeeded. Apart from these considerations, war conditions forced to the front the immediate establishment of a Wage Board.

In ordinary times, the chance of obtaining a rise in wages comes to a worker when two or more employers compete for his services. It was at first expected that the drain on man-power would give him this opportunity. On this ground, the Milner Committee of 1915 decided not to recommend minimum wages. But further experience tended to show that war conditions would increasingly prevent agricultural labourers from benefiting by the ordinary laws of supply and demand. Those laws were, in fact, suspended. In the winter of 1916–17 wages already lagged behind rising prices. Yet, in the face of food shortage, the men could not strike. Public opinion would not have tolerated any stoppage of agricultural work which would have imperilled the supply of bread, meat and milk. Their strongest weapon was struck from their hands. Many of the younger men were also placed in a new difficulty by the consequences of a dispute with their employer. They were exempted from military service for work on a particular farm, and, if dismissed, passed at once into the Army. The value of labour on the land was becoming so great, that steps had to be taken through the Labour Exchanges to discourage men from leaving the industry for more highly paid employments.

In these respects the free action of agricultural labourers was seriously restricted. Still more unfavourable to their opportunities of securing advanced wages was the administration of the plough policy. It involved the necessity of flooding their market with extraneous and subsidized labour. The Government knew that it would have to ransack the corners of the country in order to supplement the labour on the land with soldiers, women, both half-time and whole-time, public-school boys, national service volunteers, old-age pensioners, interned aliens, and prisoners of war. For their services farmers paid the current rates of wages. But if no machinery had been created to regulate wages, this army of supplementary labour—eventually more than 400,000 strong—would have been, in effect, a subsidized host of " blacklegs," taking the bread from the mouths of agricultural labourers. Such a position was impossible. The establishment of machinery to regulate wages was an essential feature in the Corn Production Act. It was, moreover, necessary that the rates fixed should be uniform throughout the country. Without intense dissatisfaction men could not have been sent into counties where the lower rates of wages prevailed. In order to establish uniform rates, the machinery had to be centralized in one body. But there was no link between the Wage Board and guaranteed prices, except that both ceased to operate at the same date. The Act did not connect the two, or make the one dependent on the other. It struck no bargain with farmers.

Whether the machinery was, or was not, the best for the purpose is, of course, an open question. It accomplished its object. The Wage Board was not an unqualified blessing. It was too rigid, too mechanical and inelastic to deal satisfactorily with an industry whose conditions are so varying as those of agriculture. On the other hand, it certainly did not prove an "unmixed curse." Agriculture in 1917–19 was hampered by no strikes; it contributed practically nothing to the record of 107,000,000 days which were lost by industrial stoppages in the eighteen months of 1920 to July, 1921. The Wage Board tided the industry over difficult times; it prevented violence; it maintained the peace; it kept wages in rural districts abreast of rising prices; it stimulated the organization of workers' unions, and materially assisted the men to stand on their own feet; it brought employers and employed together, and facilitated the creation of machinery which might prove more satisfactory to the industry. The country owes a debt of gratitude to the members of the Board, who explored an uncharted sea, and especially to Sir Ailwyn Fellowes (afterwards Lord Ailwyn), who undertook the great responsibility of the first Chairmanship.

Section III

The Harvest of 1918

During the ploughing and sowing in the spring of 1917 for the harvest of that year, plans had been laid for the harvest of 1918. The original programme for England and Wales, submitted to the Cabinet in April, 1917, was conceived on large lines. It aimed at adding three million acres to the arable area of 1916. It proceeded on the assumption that the scheme would be immediately considered, that the work could be begun in the early summer, and that sanction would be obtained for the employment of 80,000 additional able-bodied soldiers on the land, the loan of 60,000 Army horses, and the provision of 5,000 tractors. On April 18, a conference was held in London with the Chairmen of the Executive Committees and the District Commissioners, at which the necessity and scope of the plan were explained by the President. They were urged to complete their surveys in order to schedule the land most suitable for ploughing. But it was not till late in June that the Cabinet was able to consider the programme. Without the sanction of the Government, no arrangements could be completed for the indispensable supply of men, horses, and tractors. Three precious months were lost. The interval of suspense was used to revise the programme. On June 14 it was issued in a modified form to the Executive Committees. It set out the increased arable area aimed at in each county and estimated the contribution expected from each. The total task was to add, partly from permanent pasture, partly from temporary grasses, 2,600,000 acres to the tillage area of 1916.

One obstacle to the progress of the campaign was the difficulty of convincing farmers of the reality of the danger. Each delay, disappointment, failure, or modification of plans, however inevitable it might be, each acre of land appropriated for aerodromes or other military necessities, was used as a proof that the position was safe. It not only encouraged farmers to hang back, but chilled the enthusiasm of the Executive Committees. From this point of view, the loss of the summer months and the delay in the sanction of the programme were serious and widespread in their combined effects. Still more paralysing was the comparative failure to supply the promised soldier labour. The Cabinet decided (June 27) that, for the 1918 programme, 25,000 men experienced in agriculture, or used to horses, and 25,000 unskilled men should be provided by the military authorities at the rate of 5,000 a week, beginning on July 7. On this decision, the whole 50,000 men ought to have reached the Distribution Centres by the first week of September. But so great was the pressure on the various fronts that, though upwards of 30,000 had arrived by December, the full complement was not obtained till late in March, 1918. Almost equally great was the disappointment over the supply of tractors. At the end of June the Cabinet called upon the Ministry of Munitions to arrange for the home manufacture of 6,000 tractors on the specification which Mr. Ford of Detroit placed at the disposal of the Government. Again the pressure of military exigencies intervened. The arrangements had to be altered, and the machines ordered in America. But precious time was once more lost. It was not till February, 1918, that deliveries began to arrive in large numbers.

Throughout, the skilled labour situation continued unsatisfactory. One bright spot was the decision of the Cabinet in June that men employed on farms " on farm work of national importance " should not be posted for service with the Colours, or called up for medical examination or re-examination, without the consent of the Executive Committee of the county. Another was the unexpected and valuable windfall of 150 members of the Metropolitan Police, who volunteered their services in their old industry of ploughmen, and, with the consent of the Chief Commissioner, were employed on the land with excellent results. But, otherwise, the effort to obtain skilled ploughmen was disappointing. Even when the promised soldiers began to dribble in, very few were found to have any experience of the plough. A training scheme was drawn up, accepted by the Army Council, and put in operation. Though many of the men trained on rapidly, the delay was unfortunate. It meant that a number of horses were held back, because there were no skilled men to take them in charge. The dispiriting effect of these delays and successive disappointments was intensified by serious troubles over meat prices. Nor had the harvest of 1917 proved so easy or so bountiful as to lift the depression. It was better than that of 1916. On the other hand, it was the most protracted of the four war years 1914–17, and the yield per acre of all corn crops, except oats, was less than that of 1914 and 1915.

In October, 1917, the ordinary work on the farms was in arrear. But the position both of food supplies and of transport was still critical. The recent harvest showed that production had seriously declined both in France and Italy ; the foreign food resources of the Allies were pooled ; and supplies of wheat in North America, which was practically the only available source, were short. The submarine campaign was still telling severely on our carrying capacity. The British losses of 1917 amounted to 3,660,000 gross tons, or, if the losses of 1914–16 are added, to a total of upwards of 5,924,000 gross tons. On the diminished tonnage which Great

Many Discouragements

Britain commanded fell a great part of the responsibility of carrying the American troops to Europe,
an estimated sacrifice in cargo-carrying capacity of
300,000 tons a month.

In the face of these facts, it was impossible to
relax the pressure of the food-production campaign.
Efforts were made to counteract the growing feeling
that the Government was not in serious earnest.
In this hope, a second conference with the Chairmen
of Executive Committees and the District Commissioners was held on October 24 in London, when
the President had the help of Lord Milner.   During
the critical months, meetings were also held by the
President in various parts of the country—at
Shrewsbury, Exeter, Truro, Darlington, Chertsey,
Gloucester, Westminster, Newcastle, Fareham,
Reading, Norwich, and elsewhere. At all these
meetings it was evident that, apart from prices,
which were not under discussion, labour was the
main difficulty. A fresh application for help was
made to the Cabinet in November. But the result
only slightly eased the situation. Four thousand
German prisoners, who were skilled ploughmen,
were transferred to this country from France. It
was not till February, 1918, that they were housed
and made available in any number. Agricultural
furloughs for three months were also granted to
1,500 soldier ploughmen returned from overseas.

These many discouragements checked progress.
The summer months had been lost ; up to the
middle of October ordinary farm-work had fallen
into arrear, and little ploughing had been done.
But the tide was turning. The pressure was never
relaxed. The activity and efficiency of the Food
Production Department told more and more strongly.
The multifarious aid which it was able to give to

agriculturists was a practical proof of the anxiety of the Government to help. It was also a source of growing confidence to the Executive Committees, who recovered their enthusiasm, and felt that they had behind their orders the aid of a powerful organization. The concession made by the Food Controller on meat prices relieved the tension among agriculturists. The advent of the rationing system convinced the most sceptical that the food situation was critical. Public opinion among farmers slowly veered in favour of the plough. Men who from patriotic motives had broken up their grass were determined that the sacrifice should be universal. Weather conditions improved during November. Before Christmas considerable areas of wheat had been sown, stubble-land ploughed, and the root crop harvested; farm-work was well advanced. During the first weeks of 1918 the weather was ideal for ploughing. Farmers seized their opportunity gallantly. They had received little of the promised help in men or machinery. But, working themselves in the fields, early and late, and strongly backed by the willing labour of the men and women they employed, they made a magnificent attempt to complete their task. Mainly from their own resources they accomplished more than two-thirds of the programme. As compared with 1916, they increased the area under other crops than grass for the harvest of 1918 by upwards of 1,950,000 acres.

As a matter of legal form, the ploughing was done under orders from the Executive Committees. Not less than 100,000 of these notices were served on occupiers. The great majority were carried out willingly. Only in 254 cases were prosecutions instituted for default, and in 236 of these cases

Hardships and Loss

convictions were obtained. The Committees also exercised their powers of grading up the cultivation of land. A strong agricultural opinion was created against its misuse or neglect. In the vast majority of cases improvements were carried out by the occupiers themselves according to the directions of the Committees. But 27,287 acres of badly farmed land were taken possession of by the Committees, and arrangements made for their proper cultivation. In the case of 317 occupiers, holding 20,197 acres, the Board determined, or authorized the landlords to determine, the tenancies, which were at once placed under other management.

A vigorous policy, persistently pursued, is bound to make enemies. Admittedly, it caused hardships and loss to individuals. Carried out on an extensive scale with the utmost speed, it was inevitable that there should be mistakes. In some districts, Committees, unable to follow the instructions of the Board and select land with due consideration for the circumstances, balance and equipment of each farm, were obliged to aim at securing from each occupier an equality of contribution. In other districts, the ploughing of pasture was pressed when the season was too advanced for the land to be cropped with reasonable prospects of success. But, on the whole, the work of selection was admirably done, and suitable land was chosen. Even where it was not impossible that mistakes had occurred, the President defended, in Parliament and elsewhere, the action of the local agents, who were carrying out a most difficult and invidious task to the best of their judgment and experience. But individual cases were made the most of in the House of Commons and the Press. Criticism was severe. It was embittered by the state of the crops during April and May, 1918, on the freshly broken land. A cold, wet week, followed by a dry, cold period, damaged the late-sown wheat and oats, and on the newly ploughed land specially favoured wire-worms and leather-jackets, which injured, and in some cases destroyed, the young plants. Weather conditions in June, however, improved. The cereal crops revived and, as harvest approached, became exceptionally promising. In the South they were secured in fine condition ; in the North the incessant rain of September and October found them still ungathered. Flooded fields and sprouted grain became a familiar sight. It was estimated that nearly 5 per cent. of the crop was totally lost, that 7 per cent. of the wheat was unfit for milling, and that $15\frac{1}{2}$ per cent. of the barley was unfit for brewing. On the other hand, the greater part of the damaged grain was available as food for live-stock.

In the wet and protracted harvest of 1918, critics of the plough policy found fresh support for their opposition. When the ravages of insect pests on the newly broken land, the damage done by the wet months of September and October, and the sacrifice of meat on the ploughed-up pasture, were all taken into account, it was argued that the nation gained little or nothing by the increase of tillage. The point is important ; it can now be discussed without heat.

The question is not entirely one of pounds, shillings and pence. Wider considerations enter into the discussion. Without the forward policy of the plough, agriculture must have dwindled under the pressure of the war. The tillage area would have continued to contract. Government intervention would not have been justified ; the land would have been stripped of labour ; and the industry would have suffered injuries from which the present generation would have found it difficult to recover. The effort made by farmers with the aid of the Government changed the situation. It aroused popular interest, and appealed to public sympathy. The national value of the industry, for the first time for many years, was recognized. The sight of crops for human food, growing all over the country in exceptional abundance, was encouraging. It gave a sense of security. Upon a people whose nerves were strained by prolonged effort, the psychological effect was important. During the anxious months of the spring and early summer of 1918, the influence was especially useful. Nor can the movement be treated as one which affected only England and Wales or even the United Kingdom. It set an example to our Allies. Both France and Italy studied our methods, followed our lead, and for the harvest of 1918 entered on a campaign of increased production. It stimulated North America to fresh efforts to help a people who were doing their best to help themselves. The Commission sent over from the United States were profoundly impressed by the changed aspect of the face of the country. Farmers at home were the butts of plenty of domestic criticism; but from foreign nations they received unstinted praise. It is often said that opinion abroad represents the judgment of posterity on events at home. If that is true, the verdict of history will be given in favour of the plough policy and of the farmers by whom it was carried out.

To purely agricultural critics these considerations may not appeal. They do not meet the allegation that no net gain in human food resulted from the increase of tillage. As a United Kingdom effort, the figures of production for the cereal year 1918–19 stand thus. Measured in quarters, the corn crops

The Food Campaign, 1916-18

of 1918 exceeded those of 1914 by 13,943,000 quarters, and those of 1916 by 15,389,000 quarters. Measured by weight, and adding potatoes, the total weight of wheat, barley, oats, rye, mixed corn, peas, beans and potatoes produced:

> in 1914 was 14,017,000 tons.
> in 1916 ,, 11,611,000 ,,
> in 1918 ,, 18,007,000 ,,

In other words, the weight of food produced in the United Kingdom in 1918 exceeded that of 1914 by 3,990,000 tons, and that of 1916 by 6,396,000 tons. On the other hand, the total weight of turnips, swedes, mangolds and hay produced:

> in 1914 was 46,122,000 tons.
> in 1916 ,, 47,526,000 ,,
> in 1918 ,, 45,488,000 ,,

In other words, the weight of food for live-stock produced in 1918 was less than that of 1914 by 634,000 tons, and less than that of 1916 by 2,038,000 tons. Against this deficit must be set the increased weight of oat-straw in 1918, which, in England and Wales alone, exceeded the decennial average (1908–17) by 809,000 tons. Making every allowance, however, for the increased supply of oat-straw and of light and damaged wheat and barley, less food for live-stock was raised in 1918 than in 1916. The hay harvest was the worst of any of the five war years, and the root crop was not above the average.

It may, therefore, be legitimately argued that it would have been more prudent to devote less land to cereals and more to fodder. But in reply to this argument, it may be said that the food value of the crops raised was immeasurably greater than that of the meat imperilled ; that the comparison of weights between corn and roots is deceptive ; that the production of meat entails the consumption by cattle of food available for human beings ; that provision was made for the deficiency of cereals which was not only anticipated but actually occurred ; that at no time was there an acute shortage of either meat or milk ; and that, if the war had been prolonged beyond 1918, a portion of the tonnage saved on cereal imports might have been diverted to a larger importation of the world's abundant supply of concentrated cattle-food. Finally, it must be remembered that the Board was acting under the scientific advice of a powerful Committee of the Royal Society, and providing the subsistence diet of a nation at war. It may be added that the maintenance of the head of cattle was a triumph of farming skill, which takes its place by the side of the addition to the supplies of cereals and potatoes.

The net results of the addition to the food supplies are thus stated by Sir Thomas Middleton. After seed and light corn have been deducted, if the whole of the wheat and barley crops, one-sixth of the oat crop, and one-fifth of the potato crop—being the surplus above normal consumption—were used for breadstuff, the United Kingdom was enabled to supply bread for the whole population for forty weeks, at the scale of consumption and on the basis of milling of 1918. In normal times, the home-grown bread supply lasts only for ten weeks ; for the remaining forty-two weeks we rely on the foreigner. Allowing for the conditions specified by Sir T. Middleton, the campaign may be said to have reversed the position.

The Food Campaign, 1916-18

To the increases from the plough must be added the harvest of the spade. From the first statement of the policy of increased food production in December, 1916, to the end of the chapter, the development of allotments formed an integral part of the movement. As compared with 1916, the number of allotments had been, as previously stated, increased by 830,000. At the same time, in a large number of the gardens of private owners, nurserymen and florists, vegetables were to a considerable extent substituted for flowers. The additional weight of edible human food thus provided cannot be reckoned at less than a million tons.

Another argument against the plough policy is that, whatever success it attained it owed to an exceptionally favourable season. No doubt, weather conditions in 1918 were better than in 1916, but there is nothing in the comparative figures of seasons to make 1918 stand out as exceptionally favourable. It was a fair all-round year, except that the hay crop fell below the average. Weather alone did not counteract the shortage of labour or the arable cultivation of land which, according to the critics, was unsuited to the plough. The improved yields were not entirely the work of Nature. Something is due, but what proportion can never be ascertained, to the marked success of the Executive Committees in grading up the general standard of farming. Something is also due to the greatly increased quantities of sulphate of ammonia, superphosphates, and basic slag which the Food Production Department had obtained, and, by the help of the Treasury, first given in January, 1917, and subsequently continued, had delivered at uniform prices to the most remote railway stations. Thus, in the fertilizer year June 1917–

Assistance to Farmers

May, 1918, 234,000 tons of sulphate of ammonia, as compared with 78,000 tons in the corresponding period of 1915–16, were distributed ; to the supply of basic slag a net addition was made of 200,000 tons ; by a Cabinet decision of June, 1917, imports of phosphatic rock were secured at the rate of 50,000 tons a month, which resulted in the supply of 770,000 tons of superphosphates, a quantity largely in excess of that available in the preceding fertilizer year.

Some share in the increase of food is due to the assistance given in labour, horses and machinery—in men, women and boys, in the training of plough-men and tractor-drivers, in implements, harness, machinery, and supplies of other essentials, and in the organization and increased number of steam-tackle sets. Something is due to the insistence, from early in 1917 onwards, on a declaration of the germinating capacity and purity of all seeds sold—a step necessitated at the time by the scarcity of the material and the consequent temptation to sell inferior qualities, but so permanently beneficial as to be embodied in the Seeds Act of 1920. Something is due to the supply of stocks of seed wheat of good cropping varieties, of 29,700 quarters of seed oats from Scotland, the Isle of Man or Ireland, of 32,800 tons of seed potatoes, of which 22,500 tons, including 13,000 tons of immune varieties, were distributed to small growers and allotment-holders, or to the provision of the chemicals and apparatus for spraying, of demonstrations of the process, and of hundreds of lectures on its efficacy against " Potato Blight." In the success of the allotment movement, again, something is due to the expert advice of instructors, of local gardeners enlisted in the work, and of itinerant lecturers sent out by the

Royal Horticultural Society by arrangement with the Department, and to the careful watch that was kept on the supply of seeds by means of periodical returns of the stocks in the hands of seedsmen.

All these and many similar activities materially assisted the bounty of Nature. They were called into play by the adoption of the plough policy. It justified their operation. Without it, they would not have existed. They were, so to speak, the compensation for control. Without this aid, farmers would have been left to their own independent resources, and the true contrast with the actual conditions of 1918 is the position which the industry would have occupied if, denuded of labour, and short of all the essentials of agriculture, it had been unable to profit by the favourable season.

Many critics pointed out that land as grass produced food which was lost to the nation when the area was ploughed and no crop resulted. Instance after instance was quoted of failure—total, partial or temporary—till the public might well have believed that there were no successes. Many picturesque statements were made in highly coloured language. Those who lost money were vocal ; those who made it were silent. Isolated examples are dangerous foundations for arguments on either side. In August, 1918, a Return was asked from the County Executive Committees, giving particulars of the croppings and harvest yields on the newly broken permanent grass-land. In March, 1919, the completed Returns were received from 58 out of the 61 Committees. Some of the facts may be of interest.

The inquiry mainly related to wheat, barley and oats. Taking the area of broken pasture as, approximately, 1,400,000 acres, the cropping was thus distributed : wheat, 250,000 acres ; barley,

Average Yields on Broken Pasture

75,000 acres ; oats, 850,000 acres. The remaining acreage was cropped, roughly speaking, with potatoes (32,000 acres), roots (5,000 acres), beans (14,000 acres), peas (15,000 acres). Other crops grown were rye, mixed corn, buckwheat, linseed, mustard, and market-garden produce.

On this newly broken land, taking the acreage as a whole and including the total or partial failures, the average yields were as follows. That of wheat was in England and Wales 31·3 bushels per acre, as compared with the decennial average for the two countries of 31·4. The highest recorded yields were 80 bushels and 70 bushels per acre. In the case of barley, the yield was generally poor, partly, perhaps, because it was so largely used as a mending crop. The average was 28·8 bushels per acre as compared with the ten-year figure of 32·44. The highest recorded yield was 45 bushels. Oats were a very good or a very poor crop, sometimes resulting in a bare return of seed. Yields were recorded of 100 bushels per acre and of 96, 92 and 90 bushels. The general average was 43·7, as compared with the decennial average of 40·3. In the case of beans, the best yield was 43·2, the average 27·5, the ten-year figure 29·40. In the case of peas, the best yield was 31·3, and the general average of 26·9 exceeded the decennial figure of 25·7. In potatoes the highest recorded yield was 18 tons per acre, and the average (7·1) was higher than that of 1907–16 (6·16). The other crops were either grown on too small a scale to make useful comparisons, or in some of them no comparative figures are available. But in the case of mangolds, the highest recorded yield was 47·8 tons per acre, the average 28·3, and the decennial figure 19·26. These results, taken separately, afford arguments to both the advocates and opponents of the plough. The man whose broken-up pasture grew 80 bushels of wheat per acre, or 100 bushels of oats, or 18 tons of potatoes, or 47 tons of mangolds, is sure to be at loggerheads with the man whose crop totally failed, or barely returned him the seed sown. But the general averages, on which the Government took its stand, show very large increases in the supply of human food. They show, also, that on the newly broken land, after allowing for partial or total failures, the yield of all the crops except barley and beans equalled or exceeded the decennial averages.

The gathering of the corn harvest of 1918 severely taxed the tenacity and resourcefulness of farmers. The Food Production Department rendered more substantial help than it was able to give to the spring ploughing. It now had at its command 4,000 tractors, more than 4,000 reapers and binders, and 10,000 horses with the necessary harness. It placed at the disposal of Executive Committees, or released at cost price to threshing contractors, upwards of 150 threshing machines. It had trained some 4,000 tractor drivers, supplied the petrol, paraffin and lubricating oil, and carried out the necessary repairs. It arranged the supply of 20,000 tons of binder twine, either home-made or imported. It put into the harvest-field a force of 350,000 men, women and boys, whom it either controlled or had been instrumental in securing. But, even taking this help into account, the foul weather which prevailed throughout September and October made the winning of the harvest a greater achievement on the part of farmers than the ploughing and sowing of the extra acres in the favourable conditions of the winter and spring. The damage done to the grain was considerable ; yet the great bulk was

Prolonged Harvest

saved in better condition than could have been
expected. In England the harvest was the most
prolonged in the decennial period (1909–18), while
in Wales its duration was phenomenal. The following figures contrast the number of harvest days in
1918 with those of 1911, which was the shortest
harvest in the period :

Year.	England and Wales.			Wales.		
	Wheat.	Barley.	Oats.	Wheat.	Barley.	Oats.
	Days.	Days.	Days.	Days.	Days.	Days.
1911 . .	28	27	30	27	27	30
1918 . .	54	60	67	66	76	86

SECTION IV.

THE CLOSE OF THE CAMPAIGN

The unusual protraction of the harvest and the
effect of the incessant rain on the condition of the
land would have seriously hampered any attempt
to extend the arable area for the harvest of 1919.
It was therefore fortunate that the President had
already decided, on other grounds, not to ask for
a further increase of tillage. In order to recall the
circumstances, it is necessary to return to the
beginning of 1918.

The question of food supplies was still a matter
of grave anxiety. In one sense, it had indeed
assumed a new seriousness ; not only the shipping
but the wheat itself were short. During the cereal
year 1916–17, there had been grain available in

The Food Campaign, 1916-18

foreign markets, if it could be safely transported to Europe. In the cereal year 1917–18, there was not enough grain in the accessible countries, if their home consumption remained normal. The United States responded generously to the Allied appeal. By a voluntary act of self-sacrifice, her people cut off a third of their daily loaf, in order that their European Allies might be supplied with bread-stuff. But though our increased production at home had made it possible to divert supplies from this country to France and Italy, both were in desperate straits. In some districts the shortage almost amounted to famine, and fears were entertained for the *morale* of the people. It is true that the shipping position was improving. The rate of destruction had steadily declined from that of April, 1917 ; the adoption of the convoy system had checked the successes of the submarine ; the monthly returns of new tonnage built were gradually balancing the monthly losses, though that position of comparative safety was not reached till July, 1918.

If the prospect was becoming more hopeful, and the most deadly risk seemed to be in process of being averted, the strain on the reduced tonnage was growing more intense. Our carrying capacity was so restricted that civilian necessities had to be curtailed. The huge scale of the war in France, the demand for more munitions and larger supplies, the maintenance of distant expeditions, the necessity of carrying drafts from the overseas dominions, the drain on merchant shipping for the naval campaign against the submarines, made ever-increasing demands on transport. At any moment the most careful calculations were liable to be upset by new calls or unexpected losses. The torpedoing of five ships in succession reduced the country, at

The Clock-work Bomb

one time, to a ten days' supply of sugar. If a larger margin of safety was maintained in other food essentials, there was little or nothing to spare. In the early weeks of 1918, the safe arrival of grain ships from Argentina was hailed with a sigh of relief. At that time "the spectre of famine," writes Mr. J. A. Salter, Chairman of the Allied Maritime Executive, "was more terrifying than at any previous period, and the cry for more ships to transport food was only one of a host of equally insistent, but mutually destructive, claims for transport." Yet, outwardly, life went on as usual ; current stocks met everyday wants : there was no apparent interruption in the supply of necessaries. The published figures of maritime losses, though accurate, were totally misleading. But men in the secret were, so to speak, always listening to the ticking of an unseen clock-work bomb, which might at any moment explode, and destroy the whole fabric of naval, military and civilian endeavour.

Between March 21 and July 17, 1918, came the five German offensives—in the Somme Valley, on the Givenchy-Armentières front, between Rheims and Noyon, on the Montdidier-Noyon front, and finally along an extended line on either side of Rheims. The last failed. But the others were so far successful that the enemy's advance brought him within striking distance of the Channel Ports, of the main road and railway communications between the British and French Armies, and even of Paris itself.

These military facts are only mentioned here in their bearing on the Food Production campaign. The demands on tonnage were suddenly intensified. Losses in men and material had to be made good on the Western front. American soldiers had to

The Food Campaign, 1916-18

be hurried over to Europe by the sacrifice of our cargo-carrying capacity. At the same time, the advance of the Germans on the French coal-fields of the North necessitated heavy shipments of coal from this country to our Ally. In this strain on our transport facilities, every ounce of food grown or economized at home was important. The production or the saving of 5,000 tons of imported food meant an additional 1,000 American soldiers and their supplies on the Western front. No one could predict with certainty how long this extreme pressure would continue, or what limits the decline in production in France and Italy might reach. As the summer of 1918 advanced, reductions in food imports were contemplated by the Governments of Allied countries. In the following October, a statement was drawn up by the Transport Council for publication at the end of 1918. For various reasons it was not issued. But it contains such passages as the following : " It is well that the public, in considering the sacrifices they are asked to make, should remember those which Germany has borne for several years. . . . The Allied countries will not be asked to suffer a reduction in food so serious as this, and such reductions as will be necessary will be made with the definite prospect of lasting only a few months. . . . If . . . the maximum number of American troops are to be transported to France before the fighting of next year, and if the supplies without which they cannot attain their full fighting efficiency are also to be sent, it can only be by such a use of ships as will necessarily involve severe, though temporary, hardships to the public in Allied countries."

By degrees, in all probability, the veil will be lifted from other corners of the food situation which

Plough Programme for 1919

official reserve has not as yet raised. But enough has perhaps been said to explain the persistency with which the Food Campaign was urged, and the grave responsibility involved in relaxing the pressure.

In the early spring of 1918, a programme of increased tillage for the harvest of 1919 was prepared for submission to the Cabinet. It proceeded on the assumption that the war would be prolonged into the following year. Much of the tillage land of 1918 had grown corn crops for two or more years in succession without adequate labour to keep it clean or sufficient fertilizers to restore its fertility. It needed rest. But if it was withdrawn from cultivation without the provision of a substitute, there would possibly be a decreased output of food at the harvest of 1919. The maintenance of the existing scale of production was, therefore, one object of the new programme. But it also aimed at increasing supplies. It proposed to add a million acres of permanent grass to the area under the plough. It was estimated that, under wheat, oats and potatoes, the additional arable acreage would feed 1,725,000 persons, while as pasture it was feeding only 175,000 persons. Put in another way, it meant a net relief to our carrying capacity of 876,000 tons, and the transport to the Western front of 175,000 American troops. In order to carry out this new programme, the requirements of men, horses, implements, machinery, fuel and oil were carefully estimated. A Bill was also drafted continuing the powers of the Board under the Defence of the Realm Regulations which otherwise expired in August, 1918.

The 1919 programme was never submitted to the Cabinet for decision. A military emergency of the utmost gravity arose in March and April, 1918.

The Food Campaign, 1916-18

Large demands on the man-power of the country were necessitated by the success of the German offensives. The situation was extremely critical. Lord Haig issued his famous appeal to his men to hold their ground at all hazards. The Military Service Act (No. 2), raising the military age to fifty-one, and authorizing the withdrawal of exemption certificates by proclamation, became law on April 18. The new powers were immediately put into force. By a proclamation dated April 20, Tribunal Certificates held by men born between the years 1895 and 1900 were cancelled. It was also made clear that this first call was only an instalment. Agriculture ceased to be a protected industry. The pledges given to landowners and farmers, on the faith of which they had ploughed many hundreds of thousands of acres of grass, were broken. On the other hand, the military need for the men was urgent and imperative. The case was so strong as to leave no choice. It was only possible to urge the inevitable effects on food production, and, when the final decision was taken, to promise on behalf of the agricultural community that the men should, if possible, be produced. One concession was obtained after prolonged discussion and negotiation. Instead of an indefinite claim on the man-power of the industry, it was agreed on May 8 that the call should be limited to 30,000 men between the ages of nineteen and thirty-one. Quota were fixed for each County and the Executive Committees were asked to select those whose withdrawal would cause least injury to the industry.

By an irony of fate, the President of the Board was charged with the duty of defending the action of the Government in the House of Commons. Nothing could show more clearly the intensity of the new interest which had been aroused in agriculture than the changed feeling of that assembly. But the argument was simple. It would be better for us at home to have to tighten our belts than, in safety ourselves, to leave our men to be butchered by German guns on the shores of the Channel for want of reinforcements.

The decision of the Government to withdraw agricultural exemptions was announced by the President at an Agricultural Meeting at Oxford on April 25. The answer given by Mr. Stilgoe, on behalf of the County, was what might have been expected. " The Government," he said, " need not fear for the farmers of Oxfordshire. They would do their last bit, and give their last ounce, to bring nearer the end of the war." In a similar spirit of determination the call was almost everywhere received. But the process of selection revealed the full extent to which agricultural labour had been depleted. The men of the age from nineteen to twenty-three, who were taken under the " clean cut " of the proclamation, numbered 15,588. All were more or less skilled, and half were ploughmen. But the chief difficulty lay in finding the 14,412 men between the ages of twenty-three and thirty-one. They were the skilled, experienced workers on whom the cultivation of the land mainly depended. So formidable was the situation that, on the facts disclosed, the Board appealed to the Government to take only the younger men who came under the " clean cut." But the military needs were too imperative. The men were, however, allowed to remain over the hay harvest, and the total numbers eventually taken did not exceed 23,000 men.

The withdrawal of so large a proportion of the skilled labour left on the land changed the agricultural situation. In the judgment of the President of the Board, it had become impossible to persevere with the proposed programme of tillage increase for the harvest of 1919. A memorandum, drawn up by the President at the time (July 20, 1918), records the considerations which influenced this decision. So far as the general public was concerned, it would have been prudent to attempt to carry out the programme. Had there been in 1919–20 an acute shortage in cereals, the Board would have been a less vulnerable target if it had tried the plough and failed, than if it had abandoned its further use without a trial. Urban populations, short of bread, were not likely to remember that the area of grass, which can be successfully ploughed and cultivated for food, is governed by the available resources of labour.

The decision had to be taken on practical grounds. As a general permanent policy, the President strongly favoured the increase of tillage. But he was opposed to using his special powers to effect a change in system on the plea of necessity, if a real emergency no longer existed, unless the gain was certain and substantial. Unfortunately many of the conditions which decided the necessity and contributed to the success or failure of the programme were uncertain. Much, for instance, necessarily depended on favourable weather in the autumn of 1918 or the spring of 1919. So also the urgency of the need depended on the probabilities of the duration of the war, and of the future stringency of the transport position. If the war was prolonged into the spring and summer of the next year, further complications arose. Fresh calls on the man-power of the country would be made, which it might again be impossible to resist. On the

other hand, there were signs that the Germans had
shot their last bolt, and that hostilities could not
extend beyond the coming winter. As regards the
submarine menace, the corner of safety seemed to
be turned. The rate of shipbuilding was increasing ;
the rate of destruction was dwindling.

The programme for the 1919 harvest, even if it
were successfully launched and carried through,
would not relieve the threatened crisis in the autumn
and spring of 1918–19. No home-grown food could
be raised on the newly broken land in time to make
good the impending temporary reduction in imports.
From his own knowledge, the President believed
that the endurance of the rank and file of farmers
was strained to the breaking-point. The Executive Committees might be relied on to do their utmost
to carry out instructions, and behind them would
stand the Government and compulsion. But if a
great mass of agricultural opinion definitely arrayed
itself against the continuance of the plough policy,
coercion on a large scale would become so difficult
as to be impracticable.

The recent call on agricultural labour had shaken
confidence. It had revived the old uncertainty.
The first decisions of the Wage Board, which came
into operation in May, 1918, added a new element
of insecurity. Farmers felt that the rise in wages
was only a first instalment. These difficulties might
perhaps have been met by such an advance in prices
as would have stimulated production. But, in the
existing state of public feeling, there was little
prospect of any such encouragement. As events
showed, this forecast proved correct. No rise was
granted in the 1918–19 price of wheat, and the
addition made to that of oats was small. With
prices fixed, and costs of production rising, there

was, unless the patriotic incentive was plain and urgent, little temptation to farmers to spread themselves in cereal production. Moreover, the programme contemplated something more than the breaking up of poor or moderate grass. It proposed to plough 700,000 acres of pasture, which was of good, though not of the best, quality. It was on land of this character that the highest results would be obtained from arable cultivation. But strong, if not organized, opposition would be provoked, unless the national necessity was overwhelming. Unless starvation was in sight, it seemed reasonable that, where land of this capital value was at stake, an appeal should lie from the selections of the Executive Committees. But legal obstacles impose delays. If speed was really essential, the drastic powers under the Defence of the Realm Act, which expired in August, 1918, must be retained. They could not be continued except by a breach of a Parliamentary bargain which could again only be carried through Parliament on the imperative plea of national necessity.

Weighing these considerations, the President decided not to persevere with the plough programme. He came to the conclusion that neither the military position, nor the transport difficulties, nor the food prospects justified the risks of a compulsory extension of tillage, which was certain to be strongly opposed, and, at the best, would not increase supplies till September, 1919. He took the view that, with the limited and uncertain labour at their command, farmers already had as much arable land as they could manage with clear advantage. He decided to rely for increased production on concentrating the available labour on the existing arable acreage, and on stimulating and supporting the efforts of

A Division of Opinion

Executive Committees in grading up cultivation. Two circumstances, the first of which was accidental —the foul weather of September and October, and the signature of the Armistice in November—subsequently justified the President's decision.

But there were obvious risks in the abandonment of the programme as well as in its prosecution. It was natural that there should be a division of opinion at headquarters. The plough policy had been initiated by the President who had created the Food Production Department to carry it out. The latter body was now fully manned, admirably organized, efficiently equipped, enthusiastic, justly confident in its powers. In favourable weather they could probably have ploughed and cultivated the additional acreage with the resources at their command. To them the President's acceptance of the refusal of the House of Lords to renew the powers of the Defence of the Realm Act and his abandonment of the 1919 programme came as a bitter disappointment. On July 22, 1918, to the great regret of his colleagues, Lord Lee resigned. He was temporarily succeeded by Sir Charles Fielding. A few months later, the President resumed direct control, and such branches of the Department as seemed useful in times of peace were incorporated with the Board.

The war campaign for increased tillage ended with the withdrawal of the programme of 1919, though Executive Committees continued their useful efforts to raise the general standard of farming. It had been launched on a sea of difficulties, and buffeted by many storms of adversity. But its success or failure cannot be wholly measured by visible results. The policy and the organization which it had created were an insurance against the prolongation of the war. Their full effectiveness was, fortunately, never tested ; but their power of expansion enabled the Government to face the continuance of the struggle with greater confidence. Very different would have been not only the prospect, but the situation, if the country had relied on an output of food which was progressively declining from the low level of 1916.

No sound argument in favour of State control of the agricultural industry can be based upon the Food Production Campaign, unless one essential feature is borne in mind. Patriotism was, throughout, the strong incentive to the efforts of farmers. It may have graded downwards from the most self-sacrificing motive to the selfish instinct of self-preservation. But whatever form the sentiment may have assumed, it supplied the spur to exertion.

The main facts of the campaign have been recorded as impersonally as possible, without, it is hoped, undue exaggeration or depreciation of its results. I may, perhaps, be permitted to conclude on a different note, and express my gratitude to the Executive Committees whose services to the nation and the industry were of the utmost value, as well as to that great body of agriculturists who, though their knowledge of the Board's difficulties was imperfect, made allowances for their existence, and gave it the help of their most useful support and practical criticism.

CHAPTER VII

On November 27, 1919, the Hall of the Drapers'
Company, in the heart of the City of London, was
the scene of a picturesque ceremony, at which
Princess Mary distributed the decorations awarded
to some sixty girls of the Women's Land Army
for special courage, skill or devotion to duty. The
ceremony marked the demobilization of the Army ;
on November 30 it ceased to exist as an official
organization. During the war women had placed
to their credit magnificent records of successful
effort. Many of these records had been more
dramatic, few had been finer in spirit and achievement than the record of the Women's Land Army.
It deserves to have its history told in detail, with
its many thrilling episodes and brave exploits.
Even in bare outline the story may be of interest.

The enrolment of the Women's Land Army formed
part of the wider movement which the necessities
of the war enabled the President of the Board of
Agriculture to stimulate. It was one side of the
effort to revitalize rural life. Few persons realize
how much the stagnation of country villages is a
women's question. Without their help every
remedy is foredoomed to failure. From most, if
not all, country activities village women had dropped

out. Nothing replaced their former occupations.
Without these interests rural life loses its zest;
it becomes monotonous; it resolves itself into the
struggle to make two ends meet on narrow incomes
and the unvarying round of household duties. The
health of the women suffers from sheer boredom.
Their loss of interest in rural life and their change
of ideals influence their men-folk, and contribute
not only to the stagnation of villages but to the
depopulation of the country-side. From this point
of view the enrolment of the Women's Land Army
and the work of women on the land were linked up
with the efforts of the Board to extend small holdings and allotments; to revive old and introduce
new industries; to spread an interest in real agricultural education; to improve transport facilities;
to train women in such domestic arts as cheese-
making, bacon-curing, or the canning and bottling
of fruit and vegetables; to encourage the keeping of
pigs, poultry, rabbits, goats and bees; to establish
Women's Institutes, with their attendant co-operative
societies and markets, and their wide freedom of
choice of corporate activities.

The larger significance of the Women's Land
Army ought not to be ignored. But, apart from
the provision of an additional supply of labour,
the object at which it was most directly aimed was
the breakdown of the prevalent prejudice that
all forms of agricultural work are degrading to
women. This was a necessary preliminary to any
successful attempt to revive rural life. In Northumberland, and to a less degree in other Northern
Counties, agriculture is still a recognized industry
for women. In Wales, where farms are small,
pastoral, and run as family concerns, or where the
men are mainly engaged in mining, quarrying or

seafaring occupations, women still do, not only the stock work, but the field work. In England generally, on the other hand, few women are occupied in farm work of any kind. Those who are so engaged do not like to own it. Rural feeling regards agricultural employment as something improper for women. No doubt this feeling was partly due to social changes in the occupation of land, partly also to historical causes. Village memories are remarkably tenacious. The abuses of the gang system of seventy years ago were vividly remembered by some, and handed down to others in as lively a tradition. Partly also it was due to the self-interest of the male labourer. His wages and employment might suffer if farmers could rely on a supply of lower-paid female labour. There is here a real danger which needs careful watching. But, whatever is the origin of the feeling, it is widespread and strong. Not only were women reluctant to work on the land, but when forewomen with some technical knowledge were required, they were unwilling to confess to any previous experience. On this side the Land Army did admirable service. They were justly and publicly proud of their work on the land. They threw into it their youth, their zest, their intelligence. By their enthusiasm they dignified it in the estimation of others. The village women who shared in the work gained from it more, perhaps, than they at once realized. Apart from the improvement in their health, it widened their interests, and broke down the monotony of their lives. The traditional feeling of degradation was weakened, if not destroyed.

From 1915 onwards efforts had been made to secure the help of women on the land. The Labour Exchanges of the Board of Trade, and voluntary

Women on the Land, 1917-19

Associations, like the Women's Land Service Corps, an offshoot of the Women's Farm and Garden Union, were already in the field. The members of the associations were educated women, specially trained in various branches of agriculture. Their efficiency won the confidence of farmers. They paved the way for others, and, as instructresses of the unskilled recruits of the Land Army, they did valuable work. Another useful body was the Women's Legion. But the number of workers was comparatively few. In the winter of 1916–1917 the urgent need of home-grown food, and of the labour without which it could not be produced, became every day more manifest. The British Isles were a beleaguered city. The drain on the man-power of the country was increasing ; more and more men must be withdrawn from agriculture. The length of the war could not be predicted. No one could foresee at what point of exhaustion the drain of male strength would cease. Unless women helped, and helped in substantial numbers, the situation threatened to become extremely critical. A strongly organized and sustained effort was needed, if the requisite labour was to be obtained.

Early in January, 1917, a Women's Branch was set up by the President of the Board of Agriculture, charged with the special duties of increasing the supply of women workers on the land, and of securing their efficiency and employment. It was officered and staffed throughout by women, with Miss Talbot as Director, and Mrs. Alfred Lyttelton as Deputy Director. The experiment was novel. It was based on the impression, possibly incorrect, that men know much less about women and their ways than they think that they know. Whether founded on a delusion or not, the experiment justi-

fied itself by its great success. There is nothing
frivolous in instancing the admirable choice of the
workmanlike yet becoming uniform of the Land Army.
Even Victorian prejudice grew reconciled to the dress
or found solace in the reflection that it was very
Greek. In January, also, it was decided to issue a
twofold appeal to women to work on the land. One
appeal was to be directed to village women, for their
part-time services locally in their own neighbourhoods ; the other was to be addressed to women in
both town and country, who had fewer home ties,
asking them to join a mobile Land Army, prepared
to give their whole time, and to go anywhere or
undertake any agricultural work at the direction of
the Board. The appeals were ultimately issued
by the National Service Department. Provided
that the appeals obtained the greatest possible
publicity, it did not matter to the Board by whom
they were issued. The National Service Department did the work efficiently. The number of
women who responded to the first appeal for the
Land Army, issued in March, 1917, was 45,000.
To the Board, and more particularly to the Women's
Branch, was left the more difficult task of sifting
the volunteers, and of clothing, training, organizing
and allocating the selected recruits. In portions
of this work most valuable help was given by the
Labour Exchanges of the Board of Trade, now the
Ministry of Labour. Ministries are perhaps inclined
to be unduly jealous of apparent encroachments
on their spheres of control. Not the least useful
of the many services rendered by the Women's
Branch of the Board of Agriculture was the maintenance of friendly relations with all the Departments with which it was brought in contact.
Collision was avoided and co-operation secured.

Women on the Land, 1917-19

Looking back from the vantage ground of achievement, it seems impossible to exaggerate the difficulties and discouragements of the task. It was said that the women would not volunteer; that if they did, they could not do the work; that they would not persevere; that they would prove unmanageable; that the moral dangers were as insuperable as they were inevitable; that the farmers would not take them on the land; that even those who were willing to employ the women would not be permitted to do so by their wives. Every one of these gloomy predictions has been falsified by results. Yet each was based on a real risk which had to be faced and overcome.

The first difficulty was the attitude of the farmers. In some cases there was unreasoning prejudice; in others, a rooted dislike to any novelty; in most, the opposition was neither unintelligible nor discreditable to the feelings of the employers. They really feared that the women might be as great pests on the land as the weeds; they honestly did not believe that they could do the work; they did not trust them to endure its monotony; they were chivalrously reluctant to ask them to do the many dirty but necessary jobs on a farm. No doubt their personal reluctance to employ the girls was often stiffened by the opposition of their own women-folk. Temporary conditions also created difficulties which were only gradually removed. Under the recruiting system the number of men who were allowed to remain on a farm was proportioned to its arable acreage or to the stock that it carried. Farmers feared that, if they engaged unskilled, inexperienced women, they would lose their skilled, experienced men. The War Office, always ready in those difficult times to help the Board in every way consistent with their duty of securing the necessary number of recruits, removed the objection by issuing orders to their representatives that woman labour was to be treated as supplementary. But instructions filtered down slowly. Some mistakes did occur. It needed many explanations, interviews and personal appeals to cancel the effect of a single error. Another difficulty was more permanent. It arose from the natural conditions of the industry. Activity on farms varies with weather and seasons. Farmers could not be persuaded to state their labour requirements beforehand, and their reluctance was increased by the supply of casual and seasonal labour through soldiers temporarily released for work on the land, or through the employment of German prisoners. Again and again the women remained idle in the depots for considerable periods of time. Suddenly the weather changed or the crop ripened. Immediately the demand for labour rose to double or treble that of the supply, and bitter were the complaints that the women were not available as and when they were wanted. The very serious difficulty of accommodation was never entirely overcome. Farmhouses are not as a rule spacious ; empty cottages were scarce ; and it is always difficult to find lodgings in a country village. Where no housing was obtainable, other steps had to be taken. At one time the President of the Board feared that he would have to put into operation his compulsory powers of billeting. In one County those powers were used to obtain lodgings for the women employed in threshing. But obviously compulsion was not likely to contribute to the comfort of landworkers. Other methods were adopted. Canvas camps or conveyance by lorries from convenient centres sometimes tided over the difficulty. It was often only possible to provide rough accommodation, and nothing but the determination and cheerfulness of the women enabled them to endure hardships which amounted to far more than discomfort.

To the village women some of these difficulties did not apply. They had their own homes to which in bad weather they could return. For the most part country-bred, they had inherited the traditions of country life. Against them, even if unskilled, farmers were less prejudiced. They were on the spot, had other occupations, and were therefore available on emergencies for casual seasonal employment. But the difficulty of obtaining their services was great. For the first two years of the war the gravity of the crisis was but dimly appreciated in country villages by either employers or employed. In these quiet backwaters the smooth surface of ordinary life remained unruffled. People scarcely knew that, on the other side of the hill, the stream of national life was racing in a tempestuous torrent of concentrated effort. Rural feeling, as has been already said, at first set strongly against field work for women. Gradually there came a change. The dearth of men became more and more pronounced. The women's reluctance was overcome, partly by their growing sense of national danger, partly by their increasing eagerness to back up the men at the front, partly by the persistent efforts of the village Registrars, District Committees and Inspectors on behalf of the Women's Branch of the Board, partly by the lead of educated women, partly by the enthusiasm of the Women's Land Army, who not only worked themselves but recruited by their example thousands of others. At first the chief drawback to the utility of the village women was their inability to give their whole time. The obstacle was overcome by the use of group-leaders or of forewomen, who made the necessary arrangements with the farmers, collected the women into groups, and saved the employers trouble by arranging the time and pay sheets, and paying the women their wages. When once the movement was under way, more women would have come out, if they had been suitably dressed and shod. Boots and clothes were prohibitive in price, even if private individuals could procure them at all. Arrangements were made by the Women's Branch of the Board which enabled them to sell the Land Army uniform at cost price to village women who had worked on the land twenty-four hours a week for a given time. Boots were bought and retailed at wholesale prices and a bonus of 5s. a pair was allowed, to all women who had similarly qualified. The numbers of women employed on the land as part-time workers was more than trebled. In September, 1918, at a conservative estimate 320,000 were at work.

It was among the whole-time mobile Land Army that the difficulties were most severely felt. In the early stages of the movement there were both discouragement and disillusionment. For the most part the girls were recruited from the towns. They volunteered with high hopes of doing work of real use and importance to the nation. To most townswomen, accustomed to constant companionship and the restlessness of the streets, work on the farm can have offered few attractions. Some may have pined for release from the nerve-shattering routine of the factory or the close atmosphere of crowded dwellings. But even to them the severance from familiar surroundings, the isolation of country districts, the physical fatigue and monotony of agricultural work,

Women on the Land, 1917-19

the very inadequate pay, the roughness of the life both indoors and out, must have been strong deterrents. The real strength of the appeal to the women lay in the patriotic sacrifice. From this point of view, though with obvious differences in degree and conditions, the life was comparable to life in the trenches. It was on these somewhat grim grounds, rather than on alluring pictures, that the first recruiting appeals were mainly based. The women were warned at the Albert Hall by the President of the Board that it was no occasion for " lilac sun-bonnets." And the attitude was that of the women themselves. Often when sympathy was expressed with their hardships, they would reply, " It's not so bad as it is for the boys at the front." With these high ideals and glowing hopes most of the women offered themselves for enlistment. Then came the disillusionment. The Army had to fight its way in a chilling atmosphere. The attitude of agriculturists was critical or indifferent ; the demand for women's labour was uncertain and fluctuating. Women began to ask themselves, Was their help wanted ? Was the work for which they volunteered really of national utility and importance ? On all sides of them they saw their friends welcomed into munitions or similar activities, paid wages hitherto undreamed of, meeting recognized wants and ascertained needs. The sifting process was drastic. Those who remained were of the right stamp, at once enthusiastic and dogged. For them the opportunity came at last. The tide turned permanently in their favour, subject to the ebb and flow of climatic or seasonal emergencies. After the summer of 1917 the demand increased, especially in dairying and stock-work. It culminated after the call-up of men in April–June, 1918.

The Change of Feeling

In September of that year the Women's Land Army reached its highest figures at any one time ; 16,000 were working on the land. If the war had been prolonged, and if the drain on man-power had continued, the President of the Board had satisfied himself that, in the last resource, women could be trained to do a great part of the work on farms ; that if more recruits were asked for, they would be forthcoming, and that farmers would not reject their aid. To those who were called upon to address country meetings during those three years, it was interesting to note the change of feeling on the subject of women on the land. In March, 1917, any allusion to it was received in silence or with disapproving grunts. Three months later, there were interjections for or against their employment. Then came an interval when the subject was received with applause, more or less slight. There followed the period of confidence, when any reference to the work of women on the land was hailed with sympathetic cheers. The final stage was reached, when the real gratitude of the farmers was expressed in the call for " three cheers for the women." The Land Army and the village women had won. Their grit and endurance had told. But it is only fair to remember that the change from critical indifference to warm gratitude followed the increased efficiency of the women. As an agricultural instrument the Land Army of November, 1919, with its accumulated skill and experience, was a far superior force to the unskilled Army of March, 1917.

At the height of the movement the Women's Branch had to deal with some 320,000 women actually engaged in agricultural work, scattered over almost every parish in England and Wales. In order to handle so large a number dispersed throughout the country, to make the labour efficient, and to secure its employment, an elaborate organization was established. Little or nothing existed. In the initial stages the machinery was put together in haste to meet an emergency. But, as time passed, it was gradually perfected till it worked with smoothness and precision.

In December, 1916, and January, 1917, the President of the Board laid the foundations for carrying out the policy of increasing the supply of home-grown food. In the first week of the new year he created the Food Production Department and transferred to it the best available strength at his disposal. Before the end of January the War Executive Committees had been set up and were at work. They were to act as the Board's agents in each County. Unless the farmers themselves were interested in the new movement it could not succeed. In delegating some of its powers to these Committees the Board relied on local patriotism and local knowledge of agricultural conditions to carry out its policy as efficiently as possible, with the help of the newly created Department. The confidence was justified by results. The members of the War Executive Committees gave their time, skill and experience without either pay or reward, and courageously faced a disagreeable task as a public duty. The same principle was adopted with regard to women. The Women's Branch of the Board, subsequently transferred to the Food Production Department, was created in January, 1917. Women's War Agricultural Committees in each County acted as agents. The members gave their services in the same generous spirit as the men, without counting the cost to themselves of time, anxiety and money. To both County Committees clerical assistance was allowed. Otherwise their work was done with little or no expense to the nation. As both organizations developed, new duties were thrown upon them, which they accepted and discharged with unfailing readiness.

The Women's County organizations penetrated to the parish and provided for the selection, training, equipment, allocation, employment, billeting and care of the women on the land. It was through their District Committees and Village Registrars that large numbers of village women were induced to work on the farms in their own neighbourhoods. Through the Women's County Agricultural Committees and Sub-Committees the local administration of the Land Army was conducted under the supervision of the Women's Branch of the Board. Applicants for enrolment in the Land Army were interviewed by District Selection Committees, with whom sat representatives of the Employment Exchanges. If the applicant appeared to be unfit for agricultural work, she was rejected; if fit and unskilled, she was sent to a training centre; if both fit and skilled, employment was at once found for her as a paid worker. In the last two cases the decision of the Selection Committee was subject to a medical examination arranged by the Ministry of Labour. The standard of fitness and health was high. Out of the 45,000 women who responded to the first appeal 50 per cent. were rejected. When medically accepted the recruit was measured for her outfit before going to the training centre or the farm. The outfits consisted of two overalls, one hat, one pair of breeches, one pair of boots, one pair of leggings, one jersey, one pair of clogs and one mackintosh. A second issue was made within the year of one overall, one hat,

Women on the Land, 1917-19

one pair of breeches, one pair of boots and one pair of leggings. The value of a year's outfit was estimated at £7. It was obtained from the War Office Contracts Department, delivered by the contractors at the Post Office Stores, Islington, where it was inspected, stored, and dispatched, as needed, to the Counties, and so distributed to the workers in each area through the Outfit Secretary and Store Superintendent (both voluntary) of the County Committees. An elaborate system of book-keeping and stock-taking insured against waste.

The training centres were of various kinds. Specially selected farms on which two or three women were trained by the farmer, practice farms on which groups of women were trained together, agricultural colleges and farm schools were all employed. The alternate contraction and expansion of the demand for women's labour created serious difficulties, which were successfully overcome. Thus in the spring of 1918 the number of women in training was between 300 and 400; in the July following the number had risen to 2,775. The period of training was originally four weeks. It meant, and could only mean, a hardening of the muscles and a rudimentary knowledge of the use of tools; the rest was learned by actual practice. The prolongation of the period to six weeks was a great gain. The advance made in the additional fortnight was clearly marked. Efficiency tests were also introduced with good results. As the movement progressed the teaching improved; periodical inspection kept it up to the mark. What could or could not be taught within the period was more clearly ascertained. As far as possible the needs of the locality were considered. Special branches were taught, such as milking, the care of horses, or tractor-driving. Thatching, in which women became very skilled, was also taught. Altogether, between March, 1917, and May, 1919, some 23,000 women passed through the training centres. The statistics of employment, though the returns are incomplete, are interesting as they show the type of work done. To take an example. Returns relating to 12,657 women, taken in August 1918, show that the work was thus distributed : 5,734 milkers, 293 tractor-drivers, 3,971 field-workers, 635 carters, 260 ploughmen, 84 thatchers, 21 shepherds ; the rest were distributed among the other branches of the industry. Besides the purely agricultural work of the Land Army, the Women's Branch organized a centre for the training of women in forestry for service under the Woods and Forests Department of the Board. It also proved desirable to prevent competition between other Ministries. The Women's Branch therefore extended the Land Army so as to include the women required by the Timber Supply Department of the Board of Trade and by the Forage Committee of the War Office. Both sections were, however, soon withdrawn, and the Land Army at the time of its demobilization was only employed in agriculture.

In addition to permanent continuous work on farms, women have been called upon to meet the demands of seasonal emergencies. Short notice was usually given, and it proved impossible to obtain forecasts from farmers of their probable needs. A seasonal Labour Committee, set up by the Women's Branch, on which were also represented the Ministries of Labour and National Service, the Women's National Land Service Corps, the University Association of Land-Workers, and the Flax Production Branch of the Board, was successful in meeting sudden demands and preventing over-lapping. Another useful device of the Women's Branch was the weekly labour chart, which it compiled and sent to every County, showing the districts in which there was a demand for labour and those from which a supply could be obtained. But in spite of every precaution the demand could not always be foreseen, and some discontent was often expressed by farmers. An illustration comes from Romney Marsh, where the farmers had asked for labour to hoe corn. Arrangements had been made to supply German labour. But, owing to the war, objection was at the last moment taken to the employment of prisoners so near the coast. At a few hours' notice the Women's Land Army was called on to do the work for a body of disgruntled farmers, who could provide no housing accommodation that was suitable in the circumstances. Lodgings were found at Littlestone ; the War Office supplied lorries ; the women were conveyed to the scene of action every day ; they hoed the corn, and did it so well that many of them were kept on right through the summer. Work of a similar nature was done by the mobile force, often on very short notice, in lifting the heavy potato crop of 1918, or in dealing with the flax crop which, at the request of the War Office and the Air Ministry, the Board raised in various parts of the country. The mobility of the Land Army again and again proved its value in circumstances of considerable difficulty.

When the Land Army was enrolled in March, 1917, a minimum wage of 18s. a week was guaranteed. The minimum was successively increased, first to 20s., rising after three months' service to 22s. 6d. ; rising after a further three months' service to 25s.

The Board's Responsibility

At this figure, or as much more as the Wage Board might fix, the minimum wage stood in April, 1919. In November a considerable number of the women were receiving wages ranging between 25s. and 30s., and some were paid on a still higher scale. To these wages must be added, before the demobilization of the Army, the value of the yearly outfits, of the railway passes, of the training, and, during periods of unemployment, of the free maintenance at a hostel for a fortnight at a time.

In taking a number of women, aged eighteen years and upwards, away from their homes and planting them on isolated farms, the Board assumed a serious responsibility. The organization therefore included provision for securing the right social conditions for the women workers. Official organizers and inspectors were responsible for the periodical inspection of all billets as well as of training centres and hostels. In each County a sub-committee of the Women's Agricultural Committee existed to provide hostels for women when temporarily out of employment, or between periods of training. Each had also one or more voluntary workers charged with the duty of looking after the welfare of the Army. Besides the district representatives, nearly every village had its village registrar, whose address was put up at the Post Office, and to whom women could apply in any difficulty. For their leisure time, recreations were organized by the members of the County Committees. But the girls were also quite capable of providing their own amusements. Their concerts, dances and entertainments stirred many a rural village out of its torpor. The break-up of the Land Army was widely regretted by country neighbourhoods to which the Land Girls gave back the lost vitality, buoyancy and good spirits of youth. In this connection may be mentioned the monthly issue of a periodical called the *Landswoman*. Started by private enterprise, and admirably edited within the Women's Branch of the Board, the magazine proved a great success. The women themselves, were invited to contribute. Some of their little word-pictures had the colour and freshness of transcripts from the actual life and experiences of the Land Army.

The organization which was considered necessary for the success of women on the land was admittedly elaborate. But the elaboration was required by the special circumstances. If the war had been prolonged, and agriculture had become still more dependent on women's labour, it could not have been regarded as excessive. It was, as it were, a *cadre* capable of indefinite expansion. The organization was also required in order to cope with the extraordinarily fluctuating nature of the demand. In one month it might be difficult to find employment for all the trained women ; in the next, every available woman, untrained as well as trained, might be employed, and the demand might greatly exceed the supply. Nor could the welfare provisions be fairly condemned as overdone. It is comparatively easy to supervise work which is concentrated in definite areas. But in agriculture every farm is a separate factory, and the workers, over 300,000 in number, were scattered in ones or twos all over the country, or were moved in groups, here to-day, there to-morrow, to meet emergencies in remote districts. Of the value of the organization to the women themselves there can be no question. Its womanly friendliness and intimacy might be illustrated in many ways. One homely instance must suffice. Through the *Landswoman* women in remote country places could get their shopping commissions done for them in London. The personal interest taken in their welfare removed innumerable difficulties and smoothed over countless troubles, which might, and did, occur among a large number of young high-spirited women, suddenly transplanted into strange surroundings. It gave to the members of the Land Army generally a kind of happy family feeling, and the most solitary girl had the sense of belonging to somebody.

Every agricultural job to which the women of the Land Army were put they tackled to the best of their ability. That they were, when they began, raw and untrained, they would have been the first to admit. But they brought to bear upon their new tasks the quick intelligence of townswomen, the enthusiasm which had prompted their enrolment, and that attention to detail which proved so useful in their work. Their willingness was never disputed even by their severest critics. Possibly, in this discontented world, the complaint has rather been that they were too eager and too willing. No doubt they often set a pace which shook the slow-moving rustic out of his habitual stride. There are scarcely any branches of agriculture to which, under the pressure of war emergencies, women did not put their hands. In so doing they were not discouraged by the authorities, because their labour was indispensable. But experience shows that there are particular branches of agriculture for which women have special aptitudes. First among these are the handling of live-stock, and, above all, dairying and the rearing of young animals. In dealing with horses their

Women on the Land, 1917-19

light hands compensate for any want of strength. They excel in milking and dairy work, and the standard of cleanliness which they have introduced is a valuable asset. A woman's secret with animals seems to be that to her they are not machines but individuals : in intercourse with dumb creatures she has found companionship ; even a sow is a " Jezebel " or an " Isabel " according to character and behaviour. In the lighter branches of field-work and of forestry women have done admirable work. On market gardens their services have been invaluable. In thatching, which was fast becoming a rare agricultural art, they have proved most proficient ; the light muslin mask which they introduced as a protection against the dust is but one instance out of many of the intelligence which they have generally brought to bear on the industry. In driving motor-tractors they have done at least as well as men. Here also light hands tell. As drivers they have shown themselves, not only skilful and enduring, but economical.

The branches which have been enumerated cover a wide field. In all of them women have excelled. There are other kinds of agricultural work in which some women have completely succeeded. But more exceptional qualities are needed. Here and there a women has proved herself to be a competent ploughman ; but on heavy land, and in ordinary times, it is doubtful whether ploughing is a suitable occupation for women. In the dearth of male labour threshing was undertaken by women. They did it well, and even enjoyed the change of scene as the machine travelled from place to place. But it is a dirty and heavy job ; it leaves the women too dependent on the driver ; and the provision of accommodation, unless the machine draws its

A Cornish Shepherdess

own caravan for sleeping, must always be a difficulty. Whether women generally are fitted to
become shepherds is still doubtful. It is not an
industry which is satisfied by the hooped petticoat
and beribboned crook of Chelsea China. Shepherds
are becoming rare and difficult to obtain, because
among men it is not a popular branch of farm-
work. During the lambing season it means ex-
cessively long hours, not only by day but by night.
At other times it means exposure in all weathers,
and dirty and disagreeable work. On all occasions
it involves an inexhaustible stock of patience. Yet
during the war women did wonders among the
sheep. The throwing of heavy sheep is a knack
which they quickly acquired. But there remained
other obstacles. During the two months of the
lambing season the shepherd must live the life of a
hermit, and be prepared to be up all night. Unless
she is exceptionally lucky in her billet she has,
when she returns for brief intervals to her empty
cottage, to light her fire, fetch the water, boil the
kettle, prepare her meals, make the bed, and keep
her rooms tidy. One Land Army woman, who was
decorated with the Distinguished Service Bar by
Princess Mary on the 27th of November, had had
charge, in these circumstances, of a flock of 200
sheep, 150 of which were breeding ewes, on a hill
farm in Cornwall since 1917. The sheep had
never, in the owner's experience, been healthier
or more free from disease, and never had a larger
proportion of lambs been reared. But during
all those lonely hours the shepherd must have
drawn heavily on her courage and endurance. Yet
she loved the work, and found in it the rich reward
of a task well done. The sheep responded to her
ceaseless care ; though not credited with high

Women on the Land, 1917-19

intelligence, they are affectionate animals with strong maternal instincts. She learned to know them all as individuals, and they welcomed her appearance on the hill or in the fold as human beings welcome the coming of their closest friends. From what I have seen of the Land Army, I believe that many had the spirit and endurance to do the same. But in ordinary times I should hesitate to recommend shepherding as an industry to any but exceptional women.

The Cornish shepherdess is the last person to think herself a heroine. What she had done seemed a simple matter-of-fact duty. The same may be said of all the other women who won distinctions. Some had gained the decoration by exceptional skill, others by the exhibition of courage, resourcefulness and promptitude of no ordinary kind in preventing accidents or in dealing with animals rendered savage with pain or panic. Here, for instance, is the record of a Land Army girl who swam a rapidly rising river, roped a cow standing half-submerged on an island, and brought her across the stream to the bank; here is another who, hanging on to the fence with one hand, saved, one by one, a litter of small pigs from drowning in a half-frozen pond; here is a third who, wheeling a barrow along a road, met two riderless, runaway horses; by putting her barrow across the road she checked one, seized its reins, scrambled on its back, and caught and held the other. Here is the case of a Land Army girl who, when a cow mad with pain after calving was killing her calf, and when none of the men would go near her, went into the box, pacified the maddened animal, and saved the calf. Here is another case. A man entered the box of a bull in order to put on its chain, he was knocked

Womanly Qualities

down, and the bull was beginning to gore him, but a Land Army girl, climbing the barrier, kicked the bull so violently on the nose that the animal backed, giving the man time to rise ; and, as a result, both escaped. The story ended in romance ; I hope both will be " happy ever afterwards."

These instances might be multiplied. Yet the girls did not lose their womanly qualities. Among the distinctions conferred was one given to a woman who nursed her friend through diphtheria in a lonely cottage, and another to a woman who trudged eleven miles through deep snow and a Northumbrian blizzard to fetch the doctor for a sick friend. One more illustration of services rendered may be taken from the great railway strike. High praise has been justly given to the transport workers who rushed the milk supplies to London. Credit is also due to the thousands of Land Army girls who, to make this possible, milked the cows at 2 a.m. instead of at 5 a.m. and did their day's work afterwards. One at least of the volunteer transport workers was a Land Army girl whose days were occupied in work on a farm. As soon as her daily job was finished, she bicycled twenty-four miles to the starting-point, and thence drove a motor-lorry to London and back, fifty-seven miles each way, and was back at her farm work the next morning, with 162 miles of road to her credit by bicycle or lorry. Other volunteer workers did splendid work ; few can have done better than this girl.

After the signature of the Armistice the Board decided that, as soon as labour resumed its normal conditions, it would be necessary to demobilize the Land Army. The date fixed upon was the 30th of November, 1919. The decision was arrived at

as

Women on the Land, 1917-19

with great regret, but it was felt that the continuance
of the expenditure of public money on outfits,
railway warrants, maintenance during unemployment, and organization would arouse hostile criticism,
and that an outcry against subsidized labour might
make the position of the Land Army impossible.

During the year's interval of peace the Army
dwindled in numbers. In the dead agricultural
months of December to February 1918–19 many
retired. But of those who were still enrolled on
the 30th of November, 1919, it was estimated
that 75 per cent. wished to remain on the land.
Of the physical advantages which women derived
from their work, their splendid appearance of fitness, easy carriage, and steadiness of eye were
striking proofs. Drawn from all classes, many
of them developed that love of open spaces and
country pursuits which makes the call of the land
irresistible. The winner of the first prize for milking offered to the Land Army in thirteen Home
Counties was, three years before, a servant in a flat
in Victoria Street, London. In one County five of
the most successful workers were either waitresses
in an underground restaurant, milliners, or ladies'
maids. In Surrey, out of 299 Land Army women,
212 decided to remain on in farm work. Of the
remainder 44 returned to their pre-war life, 33
applied for emigration to the Colonies, and 10
were candidates for small holdings. Other Counties
show similar results. In the fields hundreds of
women gained health and strength, and found the
real interests of their lives and their possibilities
of happiness.

The Women's Land Army, at the national crisis
which called it into existence, did an admirable
piece of work. They conquered the prejudices

which met them at the outset. Into farm work,
as into other activities to which women have been
admitted, they brought a reinvigorating influence.
They showed that agriculture offers not only a
possible but a dignified calling for women. They
smoothed away the difficulties for their successors.
They gave fine proofs of grit and endurance. They
rendered their services gallantly for a very meagre
reward. In all the peace celebrations their con-
tingents received a specially hearty welcome, which
afforded some proof of the public appreciation of
their work. They passed away, regretted by their
employers, and carrying with them the gratitude
of the nation.

CHAPTER VIII

FALLACIES ABOUT LANDLORDS*

THE subject given me is that of Agricultural Land-owners. It bristles with controversies which arouse many prejudices. But we can, for a few minutes, treat agricultural landowners as neither saints nor ogres, but as ordinary persons—neither better nor worse than ourselves.

Men are land animals. Their interest in land is therefore almost universal. Most people can conduct their business without attracting public attention. Not so the landowner. *His* business is always under observation, because it affects the business and life of everyone. At work, at play, at home, we cannot escape the landowner. The result is that for centuries questions affecting the ownership of land have been burning. To-day they are still ablaze.

It is a common impression that agricultural land-owners have grown rich while others remain poor, or that they are only sleeping partners in the industry, mere rent-chargers on their estates—that, in fact, they are bloated parasites. Are they bloated ? Are they parasites ?

During the last hundred years agricultural land-

* An address given at the Summer Meeting of Vacation Students in the Examination Schools at Oxford on 9th August, 1923.

owners have not grown richer. In net income
they have become very much poorer. The growth
of the gross national income of Great Britain is
in striking contrast with the stationary character
of the gross income of agricultural landowners.
The following figures are only illustrations of these
two facts. Without a complicated discussion they
cannot be made strictly comparable. In 1800 the
gross national income of Great Britain, both exempt
and liable to income tax, was estimated at
£190,000,000. In 1922 it was similarly estimated
at £2,600,000,000. Now look at the gross income
in Great Britain from agricultural land, farms and
farm buildings, tithes, manors, fines on leases, and
some sporting rights, in 1814 and in 1922. The
former year is taken in preference to 1800, because
the area of cultivated land had then become, under
war pressure and fear of famine, more approximately as large as it is now. In 1814 the gross
income from agricultural land was 42½ millions ;
in 1922 it was 43½ millions, or practically the same.
In 1814 it was rather more than one-fifth of the
gross national income ; in 1922 it was considerably
less than one-fiftieth.

The stationary character of the gross income from
agricultural land is the more remarkable because,
during this period, landowners have spent a vast
amount of private capital on their estates. I am
not considering the money spent in buying landed
property, or even the money expended on the initial
operations necessary to reclaim the land for cultivation. I am only speaking of the outlay of
private capital in equipping the land with the
farmhouses, farm buildings, cottages, fences (including gates and posts), drainage, water-supply,
and farm roads, which are necessary to develop the

productiveness of the soil. All this essential machinery of a farm is liable, like any other machinery, to wear and tear, and has to be kept in repair and renewed. The annual cost of this upkeep, including insurance and management, may be taken at a third of the gross rent.

In a familiar passage in his well-known work on Political Economy, Mill points out that the rent of a farm includes two payments. One is payment for the use of the productive powers of the land; the other is payment of interest on the capital expended on that equipment which enables the farmer to use the land productively. The landlord, he says, is entitled to charge the ordinary interest on the value of the equipment, that is, he explains, on the cost of providing equipment as good as that then existing. It will be natural to expect that the payment of interest on capital, added to the payment for the use of the productive powers of the soil, would increase the gross income from agricultural land. It has not done so. The gross income has, as we have seen, remained stationary. What is the explanation?

It is the opinion of many experienced agriculturists that, after interest on capital at the low rate of $3\frac{1}{2}$ per cent. has been paid, and the annual cost of upkeep has been met, all rent for the use of the land itself has been swept away by the fall in prices. The correctness of this opinion mainly depends on the amount of private capital which agricultural landowners have expended per acre on the existing equipment of the farms of this country.

This subject was discussed in 1907 with great care and ability by Mr. R. J. Thompson in a paper read before the Royal Statistical Society. He came to the conclusion that in 1900 the average expenditure

Interest on Capital

of private capital on the existing equipment of farms
was £12 an acre ; that interest should be charged
at 3½ per cent., then the current rate at which the
Government borrowed ; that 35 per cent. should
be deducted from the gross rent for repairs, insurance and management ; and that, on those figures,
out of every pound of rent 4s. 6d. represented
payment for the use of land. More recently the
Land Agents' Society in 1919 prepared a Return
from the actual figures of capital outlay. It relates
to 9,000 acres, divided in 27 farms of different
sizes, belonging to different owners, in different
parts of the country. It shows that £146,000 was
spent on equipping 9,000 acres, or an average of
£16 an acre. The average net return to the landowner, after deducting from the gross rent the
necessary outgoings for repairs, insurance and
management, was 3½ per cent. on his capital, and
nothing at all for the use of the productive powers
of the land.

Neither of these inquiries fully reveals the true
condition of affairs. The outlay on a farm varies
to some extent with the purpose to which the land
is put. A purely grazing farm, for instance, requires
least expenditure. Still more important is the
variation in outlay per acre caused by the different
sizes of farms. £1,000 laid out on a 30-acre farm
is £33 an acre ; £2,000 spent on a 100-acre farm
is £20 an acre ; £7,000 spent on a 1,000-acre farm is
£7 an acre. Practically all the figures quoted by
Mr. Thompson relate to farms over 300 acres. In
the Land Agents' Return of 1919 ten of the 27
farms exceed the 300-acre limit. But in actual
fact, on the pre-war figures, out of the 435,886
holdings of England and Wales, 421,314 are holdings
of 300 acres or under, and 14,572 are farms above

300 acres.   That is to say, 96 per cent. of the farms
belong to the type in which equipment is most
expensive ;   only 4 per cent. are of the type which
it is cheapest to equip.   The average expenditure
per acre is unduly lowered by the disproportionate
number of examples of large farms on which both
Mr. Thompson and the Return of the Land Agents'
Society rely.   Based on the actual sizes of holdings,
the average outlay cannot be put at less than £20
per acre.   If this is so, landowners may receive
interest at $3\frac{1}{2}$ per cent. on their capital outlay on
equipment and the cost of its upkeep, but nothing
is paid for the use of the productive powers of the
land.

Our system of agricultural landowner and tenant
thus operates as a method of cheap agricultural
credit, founded, not on State aid, but entirely on
private capital.   A lease is practically a loan of
land equipped for cultivation at a low average rate
of interest on the capital expended in equipment.
The farmer, who as tenant accepts the loan, is thus
set free to use his own capital for the cultivation of
the soil.   The provision of the capital, running into
several hundred million pounds, on which this
system of cheap agricultural credit is founded, is
one of the benefits which agricultural landowners
confer on agriculture.

Nor is it only their capital that agricultural
landowners have contributed to the progress of the
industry.   They have by their example given a
lead to advance.   Medieval barons were indeed
rarely interested in farming.   War, military exer-
cises and the chase were their chief occupations.
There were exceptions.   Edward II. was a breeder
of horses and an expert thatcher.   An Earl of
Berkeley, at or about the same time, is said to have

attended all the markets of his neighbourhood with samples of his own corn, and fumbled in the recesses of his armour for his leathern bags of wheat, barley, or oats. But the foot of the lay owner rarely fatted the soil. The best farmers were the Church-men, especially the monks. Two of the earliest treatises on farming were written in Norman French in the thirteenth century, one by a Bishop of Lincoln, another by a Dominican Friar. But the first English book was written by a Derbyshire landowner. In 1523 John Fitzherbert put his forty years' experience into a Book of Husbandry which remained for more than a century the best and most practical work on English farming.

From the thirteenth century to the middle of the eighteenth, there was little general improvement in agriculture. If a steward of a manor in the reign of Henry III. had visited a village farm in the days of George II., he would have found the same methods, the same implements, the same limited range of crops, the same quality of live-stock. Probably he would have thought the farming more slovenly, and lamented the abandonment of more than one useful practice. Yet a number of new sources of agricultural wealth had been accumulated and tested by landowners. They had, in fact, collected the material and means for a proper rota-tion of varied cropping ; they had also solved the problem of providing winter keep for live-stock, and of supplying the country with fresh meat at Christmas instead of the smoked and salted beef or mutton which were formerly the staple diet of the nation.

In both the great periods of agricultural progress —1760–1820, and 1853–74—landowners gave the lead. In the first, they were pioneers of improved practices; in the second, they were the readiest to adopt the discoveries of science. It was the union of practice with science which in the " seventies " made English farming the model for foreign nations, and founded the world-wide reputation of English live-stock.

In the disastrous period of the last twenty years of the nineteenth century, landowners also proved their value. They bore their full share of adversity. They saved thousands of farmers from bankruptcy, nursed them through bad times, and crippled themselves in the process. Few have now the means to help in the same way or to the same extent. Heavy taxation, pressing hardly on stationary gross incomes, has completed the impoverishment which the fall in prices began.

To have created an efficient system of agricultural credit, to have been leaders in progress and mainstays in adversity are achievements which can be fairly credited to agricultural landowners. No doubt their self-interest was a spur. But it is unreasonable to deny them a mixture of more generous motives. During the last century, the net income from agricultural land has dwindled enormously as compared with the increased financial resources of other classes in the country. This fact has a bearing on some of the charges often made against agricultural landowners in the administration of their estates.

One charge is that landowners are hostile to small holdings. Technically, holdings of from one acre to fifty acres are included in this class. Before the war, out of the 435,886 farmers in England and Wales 292,000 were small holders. More than 66 per cent. of the farms in England and Wales are of this size; less than 34 per cent. are above. This very considerable proportion of small holdings does not confirm the charge of general hostility. That agricultural landowners are cautious in creating them is true. They know that certain conditions both in the holding and the holder are essential to success. If all these conditions are present, a man who has an average share of good weather and stable prices ought to succeed. If any of the con-ditions are absent, or if the man has a run of bad seasons and irregular prices, he is almost certain to fail.

In the small holder's interest landowners are cautious. They are cautious also in their own. It is a matter of business. Unless they charge a very high rent, they lose money. The land must be good in quality and convenient of access to roads and markets. Often it is the very piece which lets a considerable area of moderate and indifferent land. Suppose that a landowner desires to create a small holding of 30 acres consisting of some of the best land on a farm of 200 acres, let at £1 an acre all round. The tenant naturally asks a reduction of rent on the area which is left to him. The eye, as he says, has been picked out of his farm. The landowner is lucky if he escapes with a loss of £40 in rent. Can he recover it out of the small holding ? In most cases he cannot. At present prices, the equipment of a small holding of 30 acres will cost £1,000, or £33 an acre. Assume that the rent is 30s. an acre, that is £45. From the gross rent must be deducted one-third for the upkeep. The net rent is therefore £30, or only 3 per cent. on the capital outlay and nothing for the land. The result is that the tenant farmer is disgruntled and unsettled ; that the small holder is aggrieved because he pays 10s. an acre more than the farmer over the hedge ; and that, finally, the landowner is £10 a year out of pocket.

Another charge is that of wasting land, firstly, by neglect to improve, and secondly, by excessive preservation of game. The total area of land in England and Wales to high-water mark, but excluding the acreage covered by lakes, rivers and canals, is 37,136,626 acres. The cultivated area under crops and grass, excluding gardens, is 26,025,000 acres. The area of commons, mountain, heath, moor, and other rough land used for grazing, amounts to 4,781,000 acres. Forests, woods and plantations occupy 1,884,000 acres. The remaining 4,445,000 acres are accounted for by buildings, gardens, railways, roads, and mountains and wastes not available for grazing. It is in the $4\frac{3}{4}$ million acres of rough grazing that land is to be found which might be added to cultivation. Probably between 100,000 and 250,000 acres could be thus reclaimed. If expense were no consideration the area might be half a million acres.

In bringing land into cultivation there are two processes, each requiring some outlay of capital. The first is its preparation. Roots, for instance, have to be grubbed and stones removed ; the land must be broken up, ploughed and probably marled : a portion must be sown for meadow or pasture. Almost all the cultivated land of the country has undergone this initial process. But the preparation took place too long ago to be taken into account in estimating the present capital outlay. Now, however, when the question is the expense of bringing new land into cultivation, it must be taken into account. It cannot be put at less that £5 an acre. To this must be added the cost of equipment—that is to say, the farmhouse and outbuildings, the

Land fit for Reclamation

cottages, the fencing, including the gates and posts, the drainage, the water-supply, the farm-roads. What this will cost per acre largely depends on the size of the farms into which the newly reclaimed land is divided. Suppose that a landowner decides to reclaim a thousand acres of rough grazing, let at 1s. an acre, or £50 a year, and to do it as cheaply as possible. The initial cost of preparation is £5 an acre, or £5,000. At pre-war prices the cost of equipment for a thousand-acre farm cannot be put at less than £7,000, or £7 an acre. The capital outlay is therefore £12,000. Probably there will be no rent at all for several years. But assume that 12s. 6d. an acre is obtained from the first, or a gross rent of £625. From the gross rent must be deducted one-third for upkeep, insurance and management, say, £205. The net rent is therefore £420. But the landowner has lost the £50 a year rent for his rough grazing. He therefore only receives £370 a year on the transaction. If, as is almost certain, he has had to borrow the capital of £12,000, he pays for the loan at 5 per cent. interest £600 a year, and he receives from his new investment a net return of £370 a year. He loses £230 a year.

Go one step further, and suppose that the landowner is an enthusiast for small holdings, does what, on social grounds, we should all desire him to do, and lays out his thousand acres in 33 small holdings of 30 acres each. The initial cost of preparation is the same—£5,000 ; the equipment of the 33 holdings at £1,000 apiece is £33,000—making a total capital outlay of £38,000. At the best it is moderate land. Assume that the landowner lets at 25s. an acre, and gets it from the first. His gross rent is £1,250. From this has to be deducted the one-third for upkeep, say, £412. With 33

203

sets of farm buildings the cost of upkeep might probably be more. But that point may be waived. His net rent is therefore £838, or, if we deduct the £50 rent for rough grazing which he has lost, £788. But he has borrowed £38,000 at 5 per cent. He pays for his loan £1,900 a year, and receives from his new investment a net £788 a year. In other words, he loses £1,112 a year. Comparatively poor men must set some limits to their philanthropy.

It is also said that agricultural landowners waste land and diminish food production by excessive preservation of winged game. That damage may be done to crops by winged game is not denied, and, where preservation is carried to excess, it is a real evil. But even in pre-war days, the damage done was perhaps neither so great nor so general as has been represented.

Bad farming often sheltered itself behind the alleged depredations of the pheasant. Nor does it seem, at first sight, probable that land which was worth cultivating was ever withdrawn from food production. Landowners are rarely rich enough to sacrifice a farming rent, however small, for a sporting rent of from 1s. to 3s. per acre.

Less bitterness against game preservation would be aroused if landowners exercised their sporting rights themselves and did not let them to shooting tenants or syndicates. It is not merely that agricultural landowners themselves rarely preserve to excess, either from want of money, or respect for public opinion, or regard for their tenants. It is the intrusion of the commercial element into sport —the letting to strangers and the sale of the game —which chiefly outrages public opinion. Yet even this commercial element has advantages to the country-side. Many landowners can only afford to live in their country houses by the help of sporting rents. In other cases the sporting rights secure tenants for country houses that would otherwise stand empty. Those who live in the country know the loss to the whole neighbourhood when the big house is unoccupied. There is loss of employment and wages, loss of practice to professional men, loss of custom to local tradesmen, loss to the rate-payers of the rateable value of the empty house which must be made good elsewhere. There is loss also to farmers, for the rent of the house and the sporting rights often enable the landowner to maintain the efficient equipment of the farms which otherwise would deteriorate. Even if the house remains unoccupied, and only the sporting rights are let to shooting tenants, there are still advantages. Some of the money may go to the upkeep of the estate ; keepers are employed who otherwise might be out of work ; beaters earn money at a time when cash is scarce in rural districts. And sporting rights, thus severed and let, are a valuable rateable asset which diminishes the general burden of rate-payers. They pay the full and not the special agricultural rate ; added to the rateable value of woodlands in their natural unimproved state, the rents substantially increase the assessment, and help to reduce the burden of the rates to everyone else.

Another charge against agricultural landowners is that they provide an inadequate supply of cottages, and destroy independence by attaching their occupation to work on particular farms.

Admittedly there is a lack of cottage accommodation even in purely agricultural areas. But the deficiency is greatest in urban districts where wages are highest ; it is smallest in agricultural districts where wages are lowest. In urban areas the building of small houses as a commercial speculation by private enterprise has, for various reasons, been checked. But on agricultural land cottages are very rarely built as a commercial speculation either for sale for profit, or as a remunerative investment. They are built by agricultural landowners because they recognize a duty to house the labour employed on their land. They build them also in their own interest. Without accommodation for the workers farms could not be let. The better the provision of good cottages, the better the class of farmer and of worker that the farm will attract. Apart from questions of water-supply or of distance from school, the sites of cottages are chosen so that men in charge of animals may be on the spot, and that other workers may be as near their work as possible. There are no trams or omnibuses in agricultural districts. This is the reason why the occupation of cottages is attached to employment on particular farms. And the system cuts both ways. A man who removes to work on another farm is reasonably sure to find a vacant cottage near the scene of his labour.

Nor are agricultural workers the only occupants of houses tied to the discharge of a particular duty. Archbishops of Canterbury, Prime Ministers, Chancellors of the Exchequer, First Lords of the Admiralty, all live in tied houses. In rural villages the position is still more common ; it is more the rule than the exception. Every tenant farmer, most land agents, all woodmen, keepers, gardeners, rural postmen, policemen, and road-men, lose their local homes if they lose their local job.

Still, the system is not ideal. In towns, men may lose their employment in a particular factory, but they retain their homes. In agricultural districts, workers lose both together : they depend, in most cases, on their employers both for wages and house. I wish that I could see any practical substitute for the existing system. On the estates on which I worked for many years, the cottages were not let to farmers who sublet to the men they employed ; they were let direct to the workers by the land-owner. The system gave no greater security of tenure to the worker. When a farmer dismissed a man, the Estate Office always gave the necessary notice to quit. But it had advantages. Workers, I think, liked to feel that one man paid their wages and another let them their cottage. Apart from this sentiment, cottagers found it easier to get repairs done or a smoky chimney corrected, and it made, though slightly, for permanence because no farmer likes to be known to his landlord as unable to keep his men. The system of direct letting by the land-owner is more frequently adopted than is generally realized.

I am going to offer for consideration a Return made to the Land Agents' Society in 1914 relating to 22,727 cottages. They are not selected ; they are on different properties ; and they cover practically all the counties in England and Wales. But in fairness I must warn you that they may not be a perfectly fair sample. They are on large estates, and, however objectionable large estates may be, they are probably better equipped with cottages than most smaller properties.

There are then 22,727 cottages, built by agricultural landowners out of their own money to house the agricultural labour employed on their estates. Of them only 13,200 are occupied by the agricultural workers for whom they were intended. Of these, 5,508, or 41·73 per cent., are let direct by landowners to the occupants. Who occupy the remaining 9,527 cottages ? With one class of occupiers everyone sympathises : 3,137 of the houses are occupied by pensioners and widows. Old age pensions have been an immense boon to rural districts. But their value has been greatly enhanced by the kindly feeling which has allowed old people to remain in their homes, either rent free, or at the cheap rates allowed to workers on the estates.

There remain 6,390 cottages built by agricultural landowners, as part of their duty and interest, to house the agricultural labour employed on their estates. They are in the occupation of persons employed by the Government, or by Local Authorities, or by industrial capitalists other than agricultural landowners. All these occupants are brought there in the interest and for the convenience of their employers. If these employers did their duty as satisfactorily as agricultural landowners, and housed the labour they employ, there would be little or no deficiency of cottages in agricultural districts.

One other point in this connection may be made. County Councils are now the largest agricultural landowners. On the new holdings created since the war, houses have been generally provided for the small holders. But at the end of December, 1913, County Councils had provided 12,487 holdings. In the case of 2,159, houses had been sold or leased to the Councils. For the remaining 10,328 the Councils had built 609 houses, thus leaving 9,719 of their tenants, so far as they are concerned, homeless, depending on the provision made by others.

It is sometimes said that only a sixth, or 16 per cent., of the cottages in rural districts have gardens of more than an eighth of an acre. That state ment is not confirmed by the Return of the Land Agents' Society. It shows that out of the 22,727 cottages, 6,350 have gardens of less than an eighth of an acre, and 16,377 have an eighth or more. That is to say, slightly over 72 per cent. have gardens of 20 poles and upwards. The fact that so many of the men have gardens at their doors is one reason why the demand for allotments is relatively small in agricultural districts.

Many other fallacies about agricultural land-owners may be in circulation. But perhaps enough has been said to suggest that they are not all bloated parasites, and that something may be urged in favour of their administration of their estates. Even if these admissions are conceded, they do not meet two other popular charges. One is that they have usurped the rights of the people and, to put it bluntly, are possessors of stolen goods ; the other is that the private ownership of land is contrary to the laws of nature and natural rights. These are large subjects. It is only possible to suggest a few points for consideration.

The origin of private property in land is lost in the mists of antiquity. Possibly it originated very largely in the right of the first comer. When wandering hordes began to settle and cultivate the soil, individuals staked out their holdings, cleared them, and grew their crops. Public opinion recognized their claim to ownership. The right of the first comer is still acknowledged every day. An omnibus is a public conveyance. Everyone has a right, on payment, to a seat. But, as the omnibus fills up, the first comers sit, the later arrivals are strap-hangers. Whether this is or is not the main source of private property in land, most people would probably agree that it has stimulated the progress of civilization. But, to-day, many think that, whatever its past services, it hinders the evolution of a more perfect State. That is not my subject. Our question is whether there is any historical evidence that the people ever owned the land of the country. Ask any of the great historians of the University, and they would tell you, and, I believe, unanimously, that no evidence exists of the ownership of land by the community, and that there is, on the contrary, clear evidence in Anglo-Saxon times of estates owned by private persons, and cultivated by tenants both free and unfree, who paid to the owners labour services, or cash or produce, for the use of the land which they occupied and cultivated in common. Under different names, and in varying stages of development, manorial institutions existed among the Anglo-Saxons, if not in the Celtic age, centuries before the Conqueror reduced them to the system which, at the point of the sword, he imposed on conquered England.

On the antiquarian side, the charge, it may therefore be suggested, fails. Private property in land cannot represent a series of encroachments on the rights of the community, unless those rights ever existed, and of their existence there is no evidence. But the charge has also a modern side. To-day the land of the country is occupied in compact blocks by individual farmers who cultivate it by the labour of wage-earning workers. This uniform method of occupation and cultivation has displaced the older system of village farms occupied and tilled by groups of villagers, which may be traced through Norman, Anglo-Saxon, Roman, and, possibly, Celtic times. Whether this displacement of collective farming by individual farming meant a change of ownership is the point under discussion. On the answer rests

Private Property and Laws of Nature

the charge of robbery. Without dispute, the village
open-field farms were occupied in common, cultivated in common, grazed in common. But to
substantiate the charge of robbery, it must be proved
that they were owned in common by the occupying
cultivators.

The change from collective to individual occupation had been in gradual progress since the thirteenth
century. The story of the transition has been
sketched in outline in the first five chapters. In
the awards of the Enclosure Commissioners lies the
best answer to the charge of wholesale robbery.
Their study supports the conclusion that the present
estates of agricultural landowners have been built
up by the prosaic and legal processes of purchase,
exchange, marriage and inheritance.

Assuming that, neither historically nor legally,
can agricultural landowners be convicted of wholesale robbery, there remains the statement that
private property in land is contrary to the laws
of nature and to natural rights. This is a statement
which cuts away at the roots the peaceful evolution
of society. It starts the world afresh, and in this
destructive force lies its fascination for ardent
spirits yesterday and to-day.

If there was a body of laws of nature established
by the universal consent of mankind, it would determine many difficulties. By reference to it we could
decide what are the moral rights of individuals, and
what ought to be their legal rights. But there is
no such universal consent, and therefore the laws
of nature have settled no controversies and promoted
many. Each century has given a different answer
to the question what they are. To-day no two
communities, no two individuals would return the
same reply. Consequently, the natural rights that

Fallacies about Landlords

are supposed to be founded on these unknown laws
are only the rights which, in the opinion of the person
who claims them, ought to be recognized by public
opinion and sanctioned by law.   Evidence so vague
and contradictory affords no firm foundation for
legislative action.   Reasoning and proof are still
needed.

The plausibility of the statement mainly depends
on a confusion between ordinary laws and laws of
nature.   An ordinary law commands something to
be done or left undone.   It enjoins or forbids, and
thus creates corresponding duties, rights and wrongs.
But a law of nature only states facts.   " The earth
goes round the sun " is a fact, or, if you like, a law
of nature.   But it enjoins and forbids nothing,
and creates no rights, wrongs or duties.   The most
that can be said is that every living creature possesses
powers, faculties and capacities which correspond
with the facts or laws of its nature.   There is no
natural reason why those powers should not be
used to the full without regard to any other living
creature, and their unfettered exercise is, if you like
to call it so, a natural right.   But no one necessarily
does wrong if he hinders the exercise of a natural
right ; it may even be his duty to resist it altogether.

Tigers are carnivorous animals.   That is a fact
or law of nature, and their powers correspond to
the laws of their being.   A man, therefore, is the
God-given food of tigers.   But he has no duty to
be killed and eaten ; he commits no wrong in resist-
ing.   Which kills which, depends on which is the
strongest or the craftiest.   " Man requires food and
drink to sustain life."   That is another fact or law
of nature.   If I, hard pressed by hunger, enter your
house and eat your food, I am exercising a natural
right, even though you starve.   On the other hand,

212

Civilization and Natural Rights

you have the natural right to knock me on the head, and eat your own food, though my starvation is the consequence. Neither tigers nor men do any natural wrong in exercising to the full their natural rights without any regard to others. Morality, mercy, justice, honour, do not enter into the sphere of laws of nature. They belong to a different region of ideas. As regards tigers and men, or men and men, the exercise of natural rights means pandemonium, in which the weakest perish and the strongest survive.

Civilization controls the exercise of natural rights, so that we may live together in progressive communities. For this purpose exist our code of morality, our ideals of honesty and justice, our civil and criminal law, marriage and other institutions. Take an illustration from the House of Commons. " Man communicates thought by articulate speech." That is a fact or law of human nature, and men have the vocal organs corresponding to this law of their being. It is their natural right to use those vocal organs freely, without regard to anyone else. Every member of Parliament, therefore, has the natural right to talk as loudly and continuously as he likes. That would be pandemonium, in which only the loudest voices would be heard. For mutual convenience the members submit to regulations ; they forego their natural rights, and, except occasionally, only one member speaks at a time. In innumerable similar ways civilization intervenes to control the exercise of natural right. The policeman who regulates street traffic is, in our daily life, its representative.

It would seem, therefore, that the peaceful progress of humanity is linked to the control of natural rights. We have recently experienced what the appeal to the laws of nature means. It was by those laws, and on the assertion of her natural rights that Germany justified her war of aggression. In the public press, on platforms, in lecture rooms, in pamphlets and in less ephemeral literature, the argument was for many years developed. Germany needed more territory for her growth, and all men have equal natural rights to the use of all land. By conquest or fraud, so it was argued, Great Britain had appropriated a large part of the earth's surface. It is true that we had lavished our blood and our treasure upon our Empire; true that our possession had, in some cases, lasted for centuries; true that round it had gathered the reasonable expectations founded on a long period of quiet enjoyment; true that our exclusive occupation had been recognized in hundreds of international treaties and agreements. What do these things matter? One generation cannot rob another of the inalienable birthright of mankind. It is the natural right of nations as well as of individuals to seize and keep whatever they are strong enough to take. So a great nation turned its back on civilization, abandoned its restraints, developed what a native writer called " the beast of prey conscience " and, by the brute force of numbers in the field, claimed the unfettered exercise of its natural rights.

The example might well make us hesitate to introduce into our domestic politics that appeal to laws of nature and natural rights which, in international politics, we defeated at the cost of rivers of blood and mountains of treasure. In a country without representative institutions, governed by an autocrat supported by a military aristocracy, the appeal is to numbers in the field and the arbitrament of battle. In a democratic country, with representative insti-

Honesty and Justice

tutions, the appeal takes the shape of numbers at the poll, and the decision of the ballot. But in either case civilization demands that honesty and justice, rather than mere force of numbers, should inspire Governments, and be the touchstone of action, whether in international politics or in domestic legislation.

CHAPTER IX

FARMERS IN POLITICS*

THE subject chosen for me is a bad one for a wet day. British agriculture is not a cheerful topic; on the contrary, it is gloomy and depressing. The contrast with the brighter prospects of other countries does not help to make the position more tolerable. The industry booms on the Continent. In Great Britain, one branch of agriculture is at the moment wrecked. Corn growing is on the rocks; its S.O.S. signals are flying in all directions; no life-boats are as yet in sight. To explain the contrast between British and foreign farming, we must find the differences in the conditions at home and abroad. Undoubtedly, the principal variant is the fact that, alone among their foreign brethren, British farmers face the world's fluctuations in supply and demand. It is on this country that those uncertainties are almost exclusively concentrated. Our home market for agricultural produce, which should be the best and most stable in the world, is thus made the most capricious and the worst. It is the profitable plaything of foreign producers.

The agricultural situation is so serious that it should be squarely faced. No exaggerations are

* Written November 15, 1922.

216

Loss of Capital

needed to emphasize its gravity. The General Election will be over before this paper is printed. The subject can therefore be discussed with absolute frankness, even at the risk of " crying stinking fish."

On the heels of the drought of 1921 has trodden the fall of corn prices in 1922. Arable farmers now bear the brunt. Their financial resources are melting ; they are threatened with disaster. The ordinary crops of the arable farm, with the exception of well-saved barley, cannot be sold at a profit, and selling below or even at cost price spells ruin to business. If men are forced to go out of the industry, their capital loss at once materializes to its fullest extent. The depreciation in the value of live-stock and equipment has been heavy. It is also universal ; it hits all classes of farmers. It extends to milk-producers, stockmen, and sheep-masters, who, on the score of prices for their produce, have this year little cause for special complaint. The approximate aggregate amount of the loss cannot be put lower than 40 per cent. of farming capital, and might be put higher. In one sense, and to a certain extent, the loss is a book-keeping item. Men, for instance, who wrote up their farm horses to £80 and their dairy cows to £45, or who bought at those prices, now have to write them down to £40 and £23 respectively. But the animals remain in their possession. Unless they want to borrow or to go out of farming, the loss continues to be a paper one. Arable farmers may not be able to choose between remaining in business or retiring. If working expenses exceed receipts, a time comes when their choice is that of Hobson. Realization or borrowing reveals the greatness of their loss of capital.

Farmers in Politics

To be forced out of business is the fate which threatens the arable farmer who grows wheat at current prices and at the existing costs of production. Averages are of course deceptive; they are only the mean between high and low. It is no practical use to tell a man who wants to cross a river, but cannot swim, that the average depth of the stream is not over his head. Similarly, it is futile to console men, who have grown three quarters of wheat to the acre and sold them at 38s. per quarter, with the calculation that the average yield is four quarters and the average price 40s. Averages do not alter individual experiences, but they may illustrate an argument. The average yield of wheat per acre for the last 10 years is four quarters : the average price for the wheat of the harvest of 1922, which at the time of writing has been sold, is 40s. What has been the average cost of the crop to the farmer ? Remembering that expensive cultivations are brought into the account, it may probably be put at £10 per acre. Those figures illustrate the financial effect of the transaction. On the sale of his grain the farmer loses £2 an acre, and it is to his wheat crop that he looks for cash with which to carry on his farm. He also has his straw, which this year may average 2 cwt. over the ton per acre. If it circulates on the farm, he cannot put it higher than 30s. the ton. Where he has been fortunate enough to obtain a good sample, he will have done better on barley. On his oats he has lost, though in the shortage of hay the straw is more valuable.

Instances may no doubt be quoted of a yield of six quarters of wheat to the acre. Except on specially good land, it may be doubted whether this yield has been obtained on an outlay of £10.

Loss on Wheat-growing

In most cases the extra expenditure discounts the additional produce. Put the costs at £12, and six quarters only balance the account. At the opposite end of the scale, there are plenty of men who have only harvested three quarters to the acre, and have sold at a loss of 26s. a quarter. They could only make any profit if wheat stood at 70s. If they cannot sell their corn at a profit, most arable farmers will be puzzled to know where to look for the money with which to carry on. There is none coming in. What they have to sell has gone down out of all proportion to any fall in what they have to buy. One illustration may be given which is almost farcical. Wheat offals have been dearer for farmers to buy than the unmilled grain which they offer for sale. Wise men have fed their wheat direct to their stock, and have not played the costly comedy of buying it back at a loss after the human bread-stuff has been extracted. Nor does the urban bread-winner buy his quartern loaf more cheaply because the price paid to the farmer is back at little more than the pre-war level. Before the war, when wheat was at 34s., the 4lb. loaf cost 5d. Now, with wheat at 40s., the loaf is 9d. Who gets the extra 4d. ? It is well that townsmen should realize that none of it is in the pocket of the British farmer. In these circumstances, the corn-growing farmer, if his reserves have disappeared, must either borrow on the depleted security which he has to offer, or change his methods, reduce his labour, and let down the standard of his farming. To continue to grow corn as the staple product of his farm, on his own or borrowed capital, is, as things now are, to throw good money after bad.

If prices could be stabilized on a higher scale

Farmers in Politics

by the action of the Government, the level of farming could be maintained. To many arable farmers, and indeed to the National Farmers' Union, this is the obvious remedy. By means of a subsidy or a duty, British corn-growers should be assisted to meet the brunt of foreign competition. It is, however, a mistake to suppose that all farmers want a duty on corn. Agriculture is not one industry but several industries, and the interests of agriculturists are not always identical but are sometimes antagonistic. A pasture farmer wants cheap feeding stuffs, and does not care, so long as they are cheap, whether they are home grown or imported. But even if it is assumed that British farmers are unanimously agreed in asking for some form of protection, is such a remedy politically practicable ? The answer, in my opinion, must be an unhesitating " No."

Whatever form the assistance might take, its cost would eventually fall on taxpayers or consumers. Some people may, and do, think that the cost would not be too heavy a price to pay for increased national safety, improved national health, less congested towns, better employment, relief from the burden on the exchange, an additional guarantee of social stability. But, for one voter, whose direct interest it is that wheat should fetch better prices, there are a hundred voters to whom a cheap loaf and a reduction in taxation are necessities. A handful of enlightened and far-seeing electors might be ready to sacrifice their immediate selfish interests for ultimate national advantages, by which, in the end, they would themselves profit. But it is the mass that counts at the poll. Few voters, male or female, think beyond putting an end to war and the payment of their weekly bills.

Natural Remedy for Low Prices

Natural causes will inevitably bring the remedy. In the course of years the population of other countries will increase. Intensive, and therefore more costly, methods of cultivation will have to be adopted. More countries will consume all the wheat that they can grow. The world's exportable surplus will dwindle, and wheat production in this country will once more become not only profitable but a necessity of national existence. The process is already in operation. It is changing the volume and, in part, the direction of the streams which feed the international pool of wheat. But it has not, as yet, materially affected the total quantities or the prices of the world's surplus, which is available for export to nations that do not feed themselves. For the immediate relief of the present generation of wheat-growers, the prospect of this remote future is cold comfort. In the fullness of time the relief must inevitably come ; but its coming will be slow. Long, however, before the change has come into complete operation, and a shortage is seriously felt, prices will gradually rise towards a remunerative level.

The decrease of foreign supplies is the natural remedy for existing conditions. It is the only cure to which farmers can look forward with any confidence. Under the stress of a national crisis, the principle of a subsidy was accepted and adopted. Limited to wheat, and combined with the compulsory maintenance of the existing arable acreage, it might have been justified and retained. The experiment was not tried. The subsidy has been altogether abandoned, without even restoring the registration fee of one shilling on foreign wheat and—with some slight increase—on foreign flour. In times of peace, people's memories of past danger

and scarcity are soon blurred. England, short of
food and a trifle scared, is a different country from
England well-fed and in fancied security. To-day,
no Government, in my opinion, could attempt
to restore the abandoned principle with any reasonable prospect of remaining in power. Nothing seems
to me more certain in politics than that British
agriculture will be neither subsidized nor protected.
I fear that even the registration fee on imported
wheat and flour, though it gave farmers confidence,
brought in revenue, did not affect prices, and
would offer an inducement to inland millers to buy
home-grown wheat, could now only be restored
with difficulty and possibly with danger. Even
if in manufacturing industries Free Trade goes to
pieces under the competition of foreign producers,
necessaries of life are the very last stronghold from
which the principle will be driven. To pursue the
hope of the aid of either bounty or duty is to follow
a will-o'-the-wisp which will lead us farther into
the bog. If wheat-growing farmers sleep in their
empty corn-bins dreaming of Protection, they will
not awaken to a realization of their dream, unless
it is in a world that, like Rip van Winkle, they can
hardly recognize—a world in which sparsely peopled
countries have become densely populated.

Another much-advocated remedy must be
similarly dismissed as impracticable. Unlike Protection, it is less popular with farmers than with
their advisers from outside. It is the advice to
farm more intensively. At current prices and
existing costs of production, the adoption of that
course would mean waste of good money. Our
farmers are capable of farming as intensively as
the Chinese. They do not do it, because in present
conditions they cannot make it pay. It is sounder

counsel to advise the lowering rather than the raising of the present level of production. Unless prices rise, or costs of production fall, it is impossible for the average farmer to maintain his existing output per acre. When he cannot make money by growing more, he must save money by growing less. "High farming is not the remedy for low prices." So said Lawes, half a century ago, and the truth of the maxim has again and again been verified by experience. It is true to-day. In manufacture, large production is cheap production. It is a fatal fallacy to think that the same principle applies to wheat growing. A larger output can only be obtained by a larger outlay. Unless the price obtainable for the extra produce exceeds the cost of the additional fertilizers, the expenditure is lunacy. Our wheat-growers are knocked out, not by those who farm more intensively than themselves, but by those who grow less wheat per acre than they do—by men who average not more than 20 bushels against their 32 bushels. In such circumstances the offer of credit for the purchase of more fertilizers or for the employment of more labour would only tempt the average farmer to throw good money after bad.

If Protection and high farming are ruled out as impracticable remedies, the one for political reasons, the other on economic grounds, the result is this. So long as the nation demands cheap produce without regard to the source from which it comes, and so long as prices do not rise or costs of production do not fall, arable farmers, disorganized as they are, have only one immediate remedy in their hands. It is to lower the level of their farming, reduce their labour bills by keeping less land under the plough, and produce less food. If they cannot make a competence, they must save a livelihood. If, on the other hand, farmers were to persevere in trying to extract, even from the best land, high yields of wheat by expensive processes, we might possibly see a district like Essex again a derelict county.

Prices in the absence of legislation are beyond control. They are therefore an uncertainty. At the time of writing there is a flutter upwards. Whether the tendency is permanent, or whether it is temporarily produced by the scare of renewed war and will be followed, when peace seems again secure, by a further fall, no one can predict with confidence. I hazard no opinion. There is, however, this further consideration. When freights come down, imported wheat will be cheaper. There is also a domestic danger to our home growers of wheat which may become increasingly formidable. It arises from the growing domination of the trade by the port millers. Already it is sometimes difficult for our farmers to obtain the recognition of the parity of their wheat prices with those of foreign grain. If the inland mills succumb to the pressure of the competition, this difficulty will be accentuated. So far as his business is concerned, the port miller would be well pleased if there was no home-grown wheat. The supply of offals may be also seriously curtailed by the gradual extinction of the inland miller. In France, by the legislation of August, 1921, which requisitioned wheat on behalf of the Central Government, careful provision was made for the return of the offals to the districts where the grain was produced and for their sale at moderate prices. No such care is taken of English wheat-growers. If all English wheat is milled at the ports, what will become of the offals ? In pre-war days, large quantities were shipped from the port mills on the East Coast to our Continental rivals. I do not know whether the trade has been revived and, if so, what dimensions it has reached. The scarcity of offals in this country is partly due to the quantity of imported flour. But if, in addition, there are large exports of offals, it would explain why they have reached a price that compelled our wheat-growers to feed unmilled wheat to their stock. The point is not raised in the hope that a country so firmly wedded to its fiscal policy would interfere to restrict the trade. It is only touched on to illustrate the disorganization of the agricultural industry in the face of so destructive an engine as Free Trade.

Costs of production are the other uncertain element in the farmer's dilemma. They are at least more controllable than prices. They depend on a variety of items, small as well as large, from labour, rates and rent, down to the blacksmith's bill. What reductions can be made or help given by the Government, by landlords, or by farmers themselves ?

With the best intentions and the warmest sympathies in the world, a Government can do very little. Farmers must disabuse themselves of the idea that the Minister for Agriculture represents their business interests or is appointed for their promotion. He is a political officer, appointed and removed according to the political convenience of his party chief. He may be familiar with rural conditions and agricultural questions, or he may know little of either. But in any case what he represents is not the business of farming but the national interest of agriculture. Nearly thirty years ago, I ventured to urge that, in the long run, the creation of the Board of Agriculture would not

Farmers in Politics

prove an advantage to farmers; that it would starve their initiative; that it would lead to increasing interference from Whitehall; that it would pave the way for State control; and that, in their own business interests, they would be wiser to rely on their natural leaders as represented by the Royal Agricultural Society, or by some union of their own. As an administrative body the Ministry does excellent service in carrying out legislation, such as the laws affecting the health of animals, in collecting statistics, or in organizing education, experiments and scientific research. But it cannot be a substitute for the independent action of agriculturists. Yet the inevitable tendency of its creation was that farmers should look to it for the lead which they ought themselves to be the most competent to give. When I wrote in this strain, I little thought that I should myself wield the powers of the Board, enlarged and concentrated on a specific national object. But I have never swerved from the original opinion that Governments in this country, in normal times, are powerless to help the business interests of agriculture, and that, from a farmer's point of view, the creation of the Board was a mistake. If agriculturists had made themselves a political force, results might be different. But, disunited as they are, they are negligible at the polls.

To-day, the Government cannot impose a duty, grant a subsidy, or help in the organization of that system of co-operation which is the farmer's only defence against Free Trade. Politics forbid; Ministers are powerless. The only direct help that can be given is relief in respect of rates. Even in this direction, if agriculturists stood alone, it may be doubted whether they would obtain any measure of special relief beyond that given by the Agricultural

The Incidence of Rates

Rates Act. But on the general question of the revision of the rating system the great majority of ratepayers make common cause with them. It is not unlikely that, sooner or later, services which are wholly national will be paid for by the National Exchequer, and that a larger proportion of the cost of services which are partly national and partly local will be defrayed from the same source. When this relief comes, or when any temporary substitute is provided, there will doubtless be a flourish of trumpets. But what will it come to as an item in the reduction of costs of production ? On arable farms the proportion of the existing rates paid by agriculturists do not exceed, and are generally considerably less than five per cent. of the working expenses. The relief of fourpence per acre is not to be despised ; but it will not go far towards making corn growing a business proposition.

Neither in substance nor in form does relief of this kind meet the special case of the farmer. It does not distinguish him from other ratepayers on the ground that the nature of his business compels him to occupy a comparatively large area of rateable property. It does not recognize his plea that his land is the raw material of his industry, and should therefore, like the raw material of the manufacturer, be exempt. The analogy always seems to me more specious than convincing. The strength of the farmer's case lies in the fact that he does *not* use his land as raw material. He does not work it out in producing food, and then leave it derelict, unoccupied and no longer rateable. That would be the temporary means of reducing costs of production to which he is invited by the present incidence of the rate. So far from consuming his land as raw material, he makes a large outlay on maintaining its fertility and rateable value. In taxation the outlay on the upkeep of machinery is an allowance made to factory owners, which should be extended to farmers' rates. It would not be unreasonable for farmers to ask to set off against their rates some proportion of the money value represented by the manure and fertilizers employed on their holding, whether grass or arable. It is this outlay which prevents exhaustion and maintains the land as a rateable asset. Relief on these lines would still further reduce costs of production and at the same time encourage good farming. The political objection to its adoption—and probably the fatal objection—is that it would transfer to the shoulders of other ratepayers the burden of which farmers would be relieved.

The valuable and special help which some Continental farmers receive in transport facilities cannot be expected by British agriculturists. Our railway companies necessarily run their lines on different principles from those of Germany. Government can do little. But the law of "undue preference," as built up by a series of judicial decisions, deserves attention and possibly amendment. At present it mainly affects market gardeners and fruit-growers, whose produce is perishable and dependent for its value on freshness of arrival. But if, as at one time seemed not improbable, fresh milk is imported from the Continent, the question may become supremely important to the dairy industry.

It is only possible to state the point broadly and briefly. Foreign producers are not held to be unduly preferred by any rate for the carriage of goods which is also offered on the same or similar conditions to home producers. But the circumstances in which imported produce is received by a British railway

Railway Rates

for carriage are necessarily different from those in which home-grown produce is tendered. The foreign imports arrive at the railway siding in the docks, already collected in bulk, securely packed for transport by land and sea, and generally consigned to a more or less distant destination. They could not arrive in any other way. But on the score of these conveniences of handling, they are carried by fast trains at cheap rates. The law of undue preference is held to be satisfied if the same rate is offered to home producers on the same or similar conditions as to bulk, package and distance, or, in other words, if the conditions natural, convenient and necessary to import trade, are imposed on home traffic to which those conditions are unnatural, inconvenient and unsuitable. The effect is that the protection of the words is lost by the home producer; his natural advantages of time and distance are whittled away; and the import trade is, in practice, unduly preferred to the inland trade.

On the other hand, home growers must, of course, do their utmost to satisfy the reasonable requirements of the railway companies. They could do more if they were better organized. The point on which agriculturists should concentrate is the conveyance of perishable produce, where time is of the essence and no competition exists with sea-borne traffic. Thus limited, it is one on which the consideration of the Government might be reasonably asked, and, in view both of existing inequalities and of a possible extension of the principle, asked in the vital interest of important branches of the agricultural industry.

It is difficult to suggest any other directions in which the Government can reduce the costs of production. Little help can be expected from

Farmers in Politics

landlords. Financially, they are far more crippled than they were in the nineties. There are few rich landlords now to stand between farmers and ruin, and it is to be feared that the landlords of many of the new occupying owners are the banks. Nor is rent a really serious item in the total working expenses of an arable farm. It does not amount to more than 10 per cent., though the percentage is higher on grass. Much is said about agricultural credit, and, quite properly, various plans for its provision are discussed on Continental models. It is often forgotten that our system of landlord and tenant is an effective method of supplying credit. Tenant farmers obtain the use of the capital sunk in a farm and its equipment, at the low rate of interest which is represented by the rent. No industry commands the use of capital on cheaper terms than those which govern the letting of farms. For years past agricultural land in England has been cheaper to buy or hire than in any other country. Little help therefore can reasonably be expected from landlords in reducing costs of production, even if they were financially in a position to render that assistance.

Not only can no substantial help be expected from Governments or landlords, but together they do not represent more than 15 per cent. of the working expenses of the farm. The remaining 85 per cent. are controlled by farmers, and of the total cost from 45 to 50 per cent. is labour. In a number of details farmers may be able to effect minor savings which in the aggregate may be considerable. To attempt is particularize would be foolish. Every farmer knows better than anyone else, not only where his shoes pinch, but where they are too loose. Thrift must be the order of the day, and it is a day of small things—the stoppage of leakages, the perfecting of organization, the tightening up of administration and management, the master's eye everywhere. One special point may be noticed in costs of production. It is the blacksmith's bill. Before the war his skill was probably underpaid. To-day, he charges too much. Double pre-war prices might be reasonable ; treble are excessive. If farmers were as well organized as the blacksmiths, they would have acted instead of grumbling. Travelling forges, circulating from farm to farm in representative districts, would break rings, adjust charges on a fairer scale, and stop the irritating pin-pricks of constant overcharges.

Few people can be so sanguine as to expect that the saving on the smaller items of farming costs will, at present prices, make it commercially possible to maintain the existing level of production. If the object is to reduce expenses, the advice which is showered on farmers to use more machinery seems unsound. The value of agricultural machinery is admitted. On farms, as elsewhere, time is money, and in saving time, machinery saves money. But except in this sense, neither steam tackle nor tractors will reduce costs. Horses—never cheaper to buy than they are to-day—are still the cheapest instrument of production. Where farms and fields are large enough, steam tackle sets are universally recognized as invaluable. But tractors do not seem to be having quite a fair chance. In the last two or three years, they have improved almost out of all knowledge. The initial outlay is heavy ; the fuel is still costly, though both petrol and paraffin have almost dropped to the level of 1914 ; the overhead charge of interest on capital is large in proportion to the number of days on which the machine can be employed. But the strongest objection lies elsewhere. It is the number of break-downs, multiplied as they are by the employment of unskilled drivers, the cost of repairs, and the difficulty and delay in getting them executed. Tractors are too often and too long out of action. The objection could be modified if farmers were better organized. It is to the mutual interest of both manufacturers and users to have regional stations, for the supply of spare parts and the prompt execution of repairs, conveniently distributed in agricultural zones. If farmers combined to secure the establishment of such centres, it would materially enhance the value and reduce the cost of the tractor on the farm.

Neither minor economies nor the increased use of machinery will make corn-growing remunerative at present prices. The level of production must be lowered. Bills for fertilizers could then be cut down and concentrated on a small area of rotation crops. Large yields mean large outlay. It is only the man who lathers that can shave. When the soap has become too costly for shaving, farmers must, in the slang of the day, turn "Beaver." They must grow grass. In other words, they must either mark time with such crops as lucerne or sainfoin, or lay down their most suitable land to permanent pasture. Either expedient—temporary or permanent—means reduced employment of labour. Needs must when prices drive. When banking accounts show a debit for two successive years, few men can afford to postpone action in the only direction where large savings can be immediately effected. But farmers are placed in a cruel dilemma. It is not surprising that they should ask for a subsidy as a means of escape. Their total wages bill matters more to them than the individual items of which it is composed. That is to say, they can either reduce their staff or lower the wages all round. If men are dismissed, how are they to find employment ? If wages are lowered, how are the married men to live ? It used to be roughly estimated that the weekly wage of the ordinary labourer was a sack of wheat. At pre-war prices, wheat stood at 36s. per quarter, and on that calculation, the weekly wage would be 18s. Now, when wheat hovers between 40s. and 44s., the weekly wage would be from 20s. to 22s. Such a rate is a sheer impossibility. This is the real problem of the agricultural situation. If farmers had only themselves to think of, they could cut their coats to their cloth.

Of the two expedients that are open to farmers—marking time or the permanent conversion of tillage to pasture—it is to be hoped that they will choose the former. Prices are uncertain. They may move upwards. In that case agriculture will have tided over the crisis without the abandonment of tillage. It is in mixed arable farming for meat and milk as well as corn that, as I believe, the future prosperity of British agriculture lies. It is the national interest. It is the direction in which science is moving. It employs most labour. It makes the fullest possible use of the land. But I should hesitate to press it as a remedy for the present crisis, unless corn prices rise. More meat and milk can be raised from 100 arable acres of average quality than can be produced from the same area of the best grass. But their production is more expensive, and, unless the corn in the rotation is a paying crop, I am not sure that it is a commercial proposition.

The only business advice that, in the present crisis, can be given to the average arable farmer as an immediate remedy is to grow less food. It is a disheartening conclusion, especially in view of the consequences to labour. To the nation, unrestricted Free Trade offers advantages; but its competition in commodities which can be grown on the land of this country offers none to agriculturists. The only defence which farmers can offer to food imports is to combine in a co-operative association of growers and distributors. Each solitary farmer, standing aloof from his neighbours, ploughing his lonely furrow on his small isolated farm, pits his individual strength against the organized production of the world. If by so doing he preserved his independence, there might be consolation even in his defeat. But all the time he is bound hand and foot to the various trades and organizations which stand between him and the consumer, and live by handling his produce. It is their collective profits which reduce him to his present straits. The dividends and carry-over of commercial undertakings like the Milk Combine might open his eyes to the advantage of becoming his own distributor. Why should he not grind his own corn and sell his own offals; or butcher, wholesale and retail his own meat; or cure and sell his own bacon direct to consumers; or become his own banker and issue his own co-operative credit? By co-operative methods our own farmers could sell more cheaply to consumers, pay living wages to their men, and yet make larger profits, or profits where none at present exist.

It is only the National Union of Farmers who can start the movement with any prospect of success. It would be well worth the while of the Union to study the subject closely, to explore its all-round advantages, to test and examine the value of the weapon as a defence against the effects of Free

Co-operation

Trade. Co-operation has succeeded in this country ; it has also failed. Success or failure is due to the presence or the absence of a united body of informed and convinced opinion behind the movement. Once successfully launched, it would make converts every day. In the hands of the National Farmers' Union there is no reason why it should not triumph.

CHAPTER X

THE FUTURE OF BRITISH AGRICULTURE*

I HAVE never before addressed an audience of agricultural students. I find myself in this difficulty. I fear that what I am going to say may be to you as elementary as A B C. The unknown is always a bogy. I am ignorant, and, therefore, in awe, of the extent of your knowledge.

Your President has asked me to forecast " the Future of British Agriculture." Prophecy is easy. It is also dangerous. Fortunately for me, I am not a pessimist, and it is only the prophets of evil who catch the public eye. I can, of course, give you nothing but my personal opinions on a subject in which no certainty is attainable. The course of agriculture cannot be predicted with accuracy. It depends largely on fluctuating world-conditions. Even if it could be forecast in this country, the influence which the play of urban interests and party politics may exercise on its direction is incalculable.

I think that the future of British agriculture is bound up in arable farming—not for corn-production only, but for the combined production of bread, meat and milk. I think so for three main reasons. Firstly, it is tillage alone that can satisfy the demands of the community. Secondly, it is in the

* An address to the Plough Club at Oxford, August, 1922.

Economic Difficulties

direction of tillage that science seems to be moving all along the line, and tillage can make the fullest use, over the widest range, of scientific developments. Thirdly, tillage, for the combined production of bread, meat and milk, unites in a common enterprise the two great branches of the industry, for the increase and improvement of our live-stock become vital to the interests of arable farmers.

I shall not discuss the economic factors of the problem. They lie off the line of my inquiry, and they have been recently treated in Mr. Orwin's Presidential Address before the Agricultural Section of the British Institution. But I realize that they strike at the root of the matter. How to combine the maximum of efficiency with the minimum of cost—how to attain the desired ends of increased production with the least possible expenditure of means—are matters of extreme urgency and importance. Economic difficulties hamper the maintenance and extension of arable farming. They block the way to the adoption of proved methods of increasing the output from the land. They affect the whole range of the farmer's business. I might insist, for instance, on the value of milk-records as the only test whether a cow is paying her way, or of co-operation in buying, selling and distribution. Or I might preach the advantages of establishing, on a commercial basis, those rural industries by which, during the dead season on the land, agricultural workers might earn an adequate livelihood. Or I might urge the boon which would be conferred on agriculture if a standard of economic efficiency in organization were formulated, and adapted to varying units of land or local conditions, so as to supply a test by which each individual farmer might check the economic efficiency of his

The Future of British Agriculture

own management. Or I might dwell on the need for supplying agricultural credit, and suggest the trial of one or other of the various Continental methods. But, on this head, let me remind you that our system of landlord and tenant is, in effect, a practical means of supplying credit facilities. When a tenant takes a fully equipped farm, he virtually receives a substantial loan at the very moderate rate of interest which is represented by the rent.

Though I do not discuss the economic factors in the problem, I cannot get away from them. They crop up everywhere. They will not take "no" for an answer. They are specially important in regard to my first point. I shall steer as clear as possible of politics. But obviously, this reason for thinking that the future of British agriculture lies in tillage, namely, that tillage alone will satisfy the demands of the community, raises a number of social, political and economic questions.

The use to which agricultural land is put is no longer the private concern of owners and occupiers. It has become a matter in which the nation is vitally interested. This principle has, I believe, come not only to stay, but to exercise a growing influence. The needs of the community will have to be seriously considered. On the kind and quantity of the produce which is raised from the soil, and on the amount and remuneration of the labour that is employed, the nation will make its voice increasingly heard. Unfortunately, there is, at the present moment, for economic reasons, a sharp antagonism between the interests of the nation and of farmers. While the nation is intent on increased production, the farmer is cudgelling his brains how to make arable farming pay, and secure some return on his capital.

A Divergence of Interests

This economic antagonism cuts across agricultural operations at many points. A simple illustration is that of spring dressings of artificials on the wheat crops. Three of these dressings will considerably increase the yield of grain and of straw. It is, therefore, the national interest that all three should be applied. But the farmer has to consider the expense of the dressings in relation to the price of his produce. He has to decide whether they will cost more than the added yield is worth, whether he will give none, or stop after the first or the second. He acts accordingly. The nation asks for the maximum output ; the farmer cannot produce more than he can afford.

But the most important example of this divergence of interests is afforded by the conversion of arable land to grass. When a farmer lays down his tillage to pasture, he relieves himself from many anxieties. He lessens his pecuniary risks. He makes himself more secure of a modest return on his capital. He has not to work so hard or continuously. He produces the two commodities—fresh meat and milk—which are least exposed to foreign competition. Above all, he reduces his *total* labour bill per hundred acres, a more important matter to him than individual rates of wages, by something between a half and two-thirds. As a man of business, he is prudent ; as a farmer he is adapting himself to existing conditions. But the nation suffers a twofold loss. It suffers, firstly, from the reduction of employment and its consequences —rural depopulation, urban congestion, increased competition for employment in towns, a lowered standard of national health and virility. It suffers, secondly, from the reduced output of food. Our grass-lands have been too much neglected : they

The Future of British Agriculture

can be and ought to be improved. Sir Daniel Hall
is lyrical on lime ; Professor Somerville puts his
last shirt on basic slag. They are both right. Mine
is a different point. Suppose you could eliminate
from our poor pastures all the rush and bent and
birds-foot trefoil. Suppose you could replace them
with plenty of clover, rye-grass and dogstail.
Suppose you could raise the quality of your Poverty
Bottoms to that of those rare parcels of pasture
which are justly classed as rich. Even then, you
would be unable to raise half the quantity of food,
measured in meat and milk, which could be produced
from the same acreage of average arable land.
In 1870, agriculture fed with home-grown food
something like a third more people and employed
a third more labour, than it did in 1913. Why is
its power to support or employ a portion of the
population reduced ? In the main, it is because
we have had to turn from arable farming to grass
farming. I do not believe that the paramount
urban interests would tolerate, for any length of
time, an agricultural system which, on any extended
scale, sought salvation in the conversion of tillage
to grass, and the consequent reduction in output of
food and employment.

The farmer's answer is simple. He says that, as
a matter of business, arable farming cannot be made
to pay ; cheapness of food is incompatible with
large production. A serious question arises. Will
the ill-informed opinion of the towns have patience
to wait, while inquirers in every branch of science
collaborate with practical farmers to make tillage
a business proposition, that is to say, to make it
show profits ? I think it will. The mass of the
community are aware that, whatever changes are
introduced, the economic problem of making tillage

pay remains to be solved. If they see that a real, practical, combined effort is being made in this direction, they will give the requisite time. But the effort must be made.

Economic science will deal with the reduction of expenses to the minimum consistent with efficiency. To other branches of scientific inquiry we look for those increased yields from the soil, without a proportionate increase in the cost of production, which will give a margin of profit. So I reach my second reason for my faith in arable farming, namely, that tillage is the direction in which science seems to be moving all along the line, and that tillage is the branch of the agricultural industry which can benefit to the fullest extent, and over the widest field, by scientific developments.

Even with our present scientific resources, the prospect is encouraging. Over the whole range of plant-production on the farm there exist the widest differences between the exceptional and the average yields. In potatoes, for instance, the decennial average yield is not much over 6 tons to the acre. I do not know the highest recorded yield But in 1918, on freshly broken pasture-land, 18 tons were raised to the acre. Or take mangolds. The average yield per acre is $19\frac{1}{4}$ tons. On an acre of newly broken pasture in 1918, 47 tons were grown. Or take the three cereals, wheat, barley and oats. The average yield of wheat is 31 bushels to the acre ; the highest recorded yield is 97 bushels. Of barley the average yield is 32 bushels, and the highest recorded yield is 80 bushels. Of oats the average yield is 40 bushels, and the highest recorded yield is 121 bushels. The decennial average, of course, represents good and bad farmers, good and bad land, good and bad seasons. Between the highest record

and the average come the actual normal achievements of good farmers. They not only grumble,
but are really disappointed, if they do not exceed
40 bushels of wheat or barley, and 50 to 60 bushels
of oats. It is not impossible to raise the general
average towards the actual achievements of good
farmers, and, with the aid of science, to approximate
to the record. If money is lost or balanced on the
average yield, it would almost certainly be made on
either of the higher yields.

To what causes are the differences between these
three yields to be attributed ? To the human
agency, to favourable climatic and soil conditions,
to the use of the best and most prolific varieties of
seed, and to the adequate nutrition of the plant.
We must not underrate the importance of the
human agency. The personal equation counts for
much. Good farmers are not in the majority. We
want more men of energy, capacity, enterprise and
education, men who will build up their practical
experience on the foundation of a scientific training.
We hope that men of this stamp will be forthcoming.
Capital is, of course, a necessity ; the industry is
often, for want of it, starved. Its provision is one
of the economic problems.

There remain the natural limitations of climate
and soil, the use of the best and most prolific seeds,
and the adequate nutrition of plant life. It is here
that science has helped, is helping, and will help
still more.

Climatic conditions, especially rainfall, cannot be
controlled by human agencies. It is this fact which
mainly distinguishes agriculture from other industries. Farmers are at the mercy of the weather.
They must adapt themselves to local conditions,
humour their climate, grow the crops which it

favours, avoid those which it resents. Speaking broadly, this is the only safe rule. On this principle the farming of this country is differentiated. The wet climate of the West favours leaf production ; the drier climate of the East favours grain production. But to some slight extent, climatic conditions can be modified. They can be modified by drainage, or to a less degree by the right use of artificial fertilizers. Thus phosphates help to mitigate the disadvantages of cold and wet, while, if the climate is too dry, potassic fertilizers promote the continued growth of the plants. To some extent, also, mechanical science helps farmers to steal a march on the weather. The preparation of a seed bed, compact enough to keep the seed in contact with the soil, yet sufficiently broken to enable the infant roots to travel in pursuit of food, is obviously dependent on weather. So, also, is the right moment for sowing, on which hangs so much of the success of the crop. Few days in the winter months are favourable for either operation, and protracted harvests necessarily drive farmers into a corner. To be well forward with the autumn cultivations is an immense advantage. It gives the farmer the benefit of weathering his land by a partial fallow ; it widens his choice of the best opportunity of getting in his seed. Time is of the essence, and it is often lacking. It is here that mechanical science has already given valuable help. Tractors may not be cheaper than horse-ploughs. With the present prices of fuel and repairs they may be at least as costly. But they are as effectual, and far speedier in their working. They are also still in their infancy. Improvements in their mechanism may be confidently expected, as well as the application of their principle to other agricultural operations. Every step in these directions means greater control over the natural limitation of climate.

Another natural limitation is the character of the soil. Heavy land is favourable to leaf production, land of lighter texture to grain production. But soil conditions are much more amenable to human control than climatic conditions. Drainage, for instance, is a powerful controlling agent, by no means adequately employed. The natural limitations may, also, be profoundly modified by cultivation. In this direction great advances may be expected. The results of cultivation leap to the eye; but the precise nature of the effects produced are not yet scientifically ascertained. Cultivation is still rather an art than a science. Knowledge is control. Progress has already been made in the study of the physics of the soil. We stand on the threshold of great discoveries. We know that the soil is not a dead mass of mineral particles. It is teeming with life. In the multitudinous struggle for existence which goes on beneath the surface, each living organism influences the changes which affect the growth of plants. Science is making a determined effort to master this subterranean chemical laboratory and to direct its operations. If it succeeds —and it will—the effects may be far reaching.

Let me give you one simple illustration. Clover is already one of the most valuable of our crops. It is so not merely because of the fodder that it supplies to cattle. It is so, also, because of its peculiar power of enriching the soil with nitrogenous matter. Possibly science may be able to stimulate still further the action of the nodules at the roots in which this fertilizing power resides. But the potential value of the crop is as yet limited by two of its characteristics. It cannot be grown con-

Control of Soil Conditions

tinuously on the same land, and it is liable to more or less frequent failures, though these may, of course, be mitigated by an admixture of grass. If the study of the biology of the soil solves the mystery of the failure and enables farmers to grow the crop continuously on the same land, the full potentialities of clover will be utilized to immense advantage.

Further control over the natural limitations of soil conditions, as well as the proper nourishment of plant life, are gained by the command and right use of farm-yard manure and of artificial fertilizers.

As the best of our all-round manures, " muck " is the basis of the manuring system of the farm. Something between thirty-five and forty millions of tons of farm-yard manure are produced annually in this country. It is probably no exaggeration to say that half is probably wasted from improper making and storage. Its management is a first-class test of a first-class farmer. Whether science will some day invent a method of fixing which will prevent the leakage of the precious urine may be doubted. The clamp, properly placed and made, at present holds the field as the best preventive of waste. Again, the bacteriological process of rotting straw may be valuable where there is an excess of straw. Its cost works out, I believe, at something like five shillings per ton. But, for myself, before buying the plant I should be inclined to try a larger head of stock. Under the modern hygiene of the dairy, there is a danger that the manure of dairy cattle may be wasted. To avoid contamination of the milk, bedding can only be used sparingly and the stalls must be cleaned out at least once a day. It is a matter which has not escaped the attention of science, and a remedy will, I believe, be found.

Large as is the supply of farm-yard manure, it

The Future of British Agriculture

remains inadequate. In this respect agricultural chemistry has supplemented the resources of farmers. But artificial fertilizers are more than a supplement. Their best results are generally obtainable in combination with farm-yard manure. Few persons suppose that chemistry has shot its bolt, and that no new combinations or ingredients may be discovered. In the intelligent use of the substances already known much remains to be done. Many men still do themselves as much harm as good by the choice of the wrong fertilizers. In the saving of the most valuable properties of farm-yard manure, in greater knowledge of the use of existing fertilizing agencies, and in the future discoveries of agricultural chemistry lie great potentialities of increased yields without a proportionate increase in the cost of production. Not the least of the advantages of improved machinery and implements and of the greater command of fertilizing agencies, is the freedom which they confer on farmers from the too rigid tyranny of rotations and the necessity of fallows. Weeds can be rapidly eradicated by the one, and fertility maintained by the other, with the result that the same crops can be grown continuously on the same land.

Increased control over climate by the use of improved machinery, increased control of soil conditions as the result of the study of the physics of the soil, increased control of the foods appropriate to plant nutrition, are important steps in raising average yields towards the highest recorded yields. Another step is the increased command and use of the most prolific varieties of seeds. Plant-breeding is the fairyland of agricultural science. No limit can be set to the possibilities in store, especially with the aid of a deeper knowledge of the physics of the soil. One example may illustrate the value of this collaboration. One serious difficulty in introducing the most prolific varieties is the weakness of the stem. The strength of the straw is only in part dependent on the plant itself. Another part depends on soil conditions. Solve that mystery and the plant breeder will do the rest. Nor must the work of the plant pathologist be forgotten in the cure or prevention of plant diseases from a variety of causes. The annual loss from these pests is very large. I cannot vouch for the figure, but I have heard it estimated at twenty-seven million pounds a year. It may bring home to us the magnitude of this sum if we remember that it is, approximately, the net annual cash value to the farmer of his sales of the wheat and potato crops of the United Kingdom.

I have touched on a few of the ways in which science is helping to make arable farming a business proposition. I do not say that science has nothing to offer grass-farmers. It has much. But I have, I hope, shown that it is tillage which can profit most and over the widest range by scientific developments. You may, however, quite rightly remind me of the natural limitations imposed by climate and soil. You may ask, with reason, do not rainfall and heavy land restrict arable farming to the dry climate and the soils of lighter texture. I do not think so. So I reach my third and last reason for my faith in tillage. Neither a moist climate nor a heavy soil restrict farmers to grass. There are arable crops which are equally adapted to these natural conditions, equally suited for the summer production of meat and milk, superior to pasture in supply of winter food, and yielding a much greater weight of fodder all the year round. Such are seeds, mangolds, vetches, peas, kale, rape and combinations of crops like oats and tares, or oats and peas, or rye and vetches. Some can be fed direct in winter ; some can be turned into hay or ensilage for winter use ; others can be fed green in the summer. Such a system lends itself to great extension and development. It reduces to a minimum the ration of roots, which, on the decennial average of a yield of under fourteen tons to the acre, are absolutely ruinous to produce. It makes it possible to carry on three acres, two cows instead of one, maintain them in good health, and obtain an increased yield of milk. Keep your eyes open for the Reports of the Harper Adams College, and study the system wherever you find it even partially adopted.

Meanwhile, let me point out the features in which the system satisfies some of the requirements of which I have been speaking. It satisfies the demands of the community, for it produces per acre more food and employs more labour than grass. It profits by all the aid that science can render in the directions which we have traversed. It enables a heavier head of stock to be carried, whether for the dairy or the butcher, than can be carried on grass, and thus unites the corn-growing and live-stock industries in one common enterprise. It can utilize all that science may have to teach on the improvement of live-stock for the various purposes for which they are bred, on their most economic yet efficient feeding, on their protection or cure from disease. It will give farmers command of more manure, and of richer manure, because it will be derived, not only from young growing animals, but from dairy cattle and, still more, from fatting beasts. It sets in motion the familiar round of the more fodder, the more stock ; the more stock,

The Oxford Plough Club

the more manure ; the more manure, the more
fodder crops.

These are the main reasons why I think that the
future of British agriculture is bound up, sooner or
later, and, in my belief, sooner rather than later, in
arable farming.

May I close on a different note ? I accepted your
President's invitation because, as the Minister in
office when your school was established, I take a
semi-fatherly interest in the success of your agricultural course and am convinced of its value to the
country. Men of education, capacity and initiative
are needed in the industry. For you there is a place
and a lead, if you will qualify to take the one and
give the other. Fortunes may be rarely made in
farming. But I know few careers which are fuller
of varied interests, few in which you can so long
continue to learn, few which are richer in opportunities of service to your fellow men. I wish long
life and prosperity to the Oxford Plough Club.

INDEX

Index

Index

of Arches, 89; Frampton's, 89; New College Manor, 89; clothier industry (1450–1560), 91; compensation for enclosures, 94; success of change, 94; stage coaches to motor bus, 95

Ellis, William, 38, 46, 49, 51

Enclosures, beginning of, 15; raise popular passion, 15; industrial prosperity involved, 16; motives for, 21; sheep farming and wool, 22; meaning of "farm," 23; recognized by Act of Parliament, 24, 29; proceedings for securing, 57; increase of freeholders, 58; results of Enclosure Acts, 59, 61; owner and tenant, 61–62; at East Hendred, 91, 93

Engrossing, 23

Exchange of holdings, 13

Eyston, Basil, 93

Eyston, Charles, 79

" FARM," meaning of, 23

Farmer, S. W., 113

Farming, British and foreign, 216; fall of corn prices, 217; depreciation of live-stock, 217; average yield per acre, 218; Protection not politically practicable, 220; cheap loaf and reduced taxation necessary, 220; decreased foreign supplies remedy, 221; registration fee result, 222; intensive farming, 222; not economical remedy, 223;

lower level of farming, 223; prices beyond control, 224; lower freights, 224; port millers, 224; supply of offals, 224; imported flour, 225; costs of production, 225; Minister for Agriculture, 225; political, not business, 226; co-operation against Free Trade, 226; Agricultural Rates Act, 227; necessity for allowance for fertilizing, 228; Continental farmers, transport facilities, 228; "undue preference," 228; no help from landlords, 230; reduce working expenses, 230; blacksmiths' charges excessive, 231; horses cheap, 231; tractors, 231; lower production, 232; mixed arable farming remedy, 233; grow less food, 234; co-operation of growers and distributors, 234; National Union of Farmers, 234; defence against Free Trade, 234

Fellowes, Sir Ailwyn, 141

Fertilizers, list of, 45–46; essential elements of, 47; gypsum, 49; soot, 49; seaweed, 50; potash, 50–51; Strassfurt deposits, 51; increase in, 153

Feudal system breaking up, 13, 21

Fielding, Sir Charles, 167

Fitzherbert, John, 34; advocates enclosures, 35; mixed husbandry, 35, 42, 48, 199

Floud, Sir Francis, 112

253

Index

Food Campaign (1916–18), 99
et seq.: War Agricultural
Committees, 106; Sir Mark
Collet, 106; District Committees, 109; grouping of Counties, 109; Cultivation of Lands
Order, 110; Food Production
Department, 111; divisions
of, 112; Advisory Committee,
112; interests of consumers,
114–123; shortage of labour,
124; new agricultural army,
125; old age pensioners, 127;
prisoners of war, 127; interned aliens, 127; Land
Army, 128; National Service
Department, 129; the 1917
harvest, 131; increased tillage
area, 131; live-stock and tillage, 133; hops and brewing,
135; reduction of bulb-growing, 136; increase of allotments, 136–137; pig keeping,
137–138; Corn Production
Bill (1917), 138; Wage Board,
139; Sir Ailwyn Fellowes,
141; harvest of 1918, 141;
labour difficulty, 145;
farmers' assistance, 146; increased area of crops, 146;
Allies followed our lead, 149;
comparison of crops yielded,
150; spade harvest, 152; increase in fertilizers, 153; Seeds
Act, 1920; yield of broken
pasture, 154–156; U. S. assistance, 158; "Spectre of
Famine," 159; strain on transport facilities, 160; Transport Council statement, 160;
military need for men, 162;

Military Service Act (No. 2),
162; agricultural exemptions
withdrawn, 163; extension of
tillage abandoned, 166; grad-
ing up cultivation, 167
Food Production Department,
111
Forbes, Archibald, 67
Forestry and forage, Land
Army, 183
Frampton's, 89
Freeholders, 7
Free Trade and farmers, 226,
234

GAME preservation, 204
Googe, Barnabe (1577), 38;
rape, trefoil, turnips, 38, 42, 48
Goschen, Lord, 112
Grazing rights, 6
Green manuring, 37, 46; ruck-
wheat, 37; tares, 37; lupins,
37, 46
Gypsum, 49

HAIG, Lord, appeal to his men,
162
Hall, Sir Daniel, on lime, 240
Harper Adams College, 248
Harvest (1917), 131; (1918), 141
Home occupations in villages, 81
Hopkins, Richard, 93
Hops, 135
Horses, cheap, 231
Houghton, Michael (1700), 41
Howet, Cromwell, turnips, 40

IMPORTED flour, 225
Increase of allotments, 136
Individual tenancies, advan-
tages of, 31, 92

Index

255

Index

Index

copyholders, 7 ; lease-holders, 7 ; yearly tenants, 7 ; rents by military service, 7 ; team labour, 7 ; manual labour, 7 ; money rents, 7 ; each village self-supporting, 8 ; no demand for agricultural produce, 8 ; rigid rules, 10 ; compulsory triennial succession, 10 ; drainage impossible, 10 ; manure inadequate, 10 ; live-stock ill-fed, 11 ; enclosures remedy, 11 ; decline in productivity, 11 ; exchange of holdings, 13 ; landless labourers for hire, 13 ; paying rent by labour, 13 ; farming-practices in disuse, 14 ; conversion of holdings, 14, 19 ; meaning of "farm," 23 ; old system breaking down, 25 ; practically disappeared in 1815, 29 ; obstacles to progress, 31 ; organization broken up, 60 ; drastic change demanded, 92, 95 ; local industries destroyed, 96 ; farm-workers insecure, 96 ; comparison with France and Germany, 96–98

WAGE Board, 139
Wages, Land Army, 184
War Agricultural Committees, 106, 180
Weaver, Sir Lawrence, 112

Weston, Sir Richard (1648), 40
Wheat, price of, 22 ; average yield, 25, 241
Women's Land Army, 169 *et seq.* : prevalent prejudices, 170 ; competition with male labourer, 171 ; uniforms, 173 ; selecting recruits, 173 ; treated as supplementary, 175 ; accommodation difficulty, 175 ; part-time workers, 177 ; drastic sifting out, 178 ; demand increased with efficiency, 179 ; Women's War Agricultural Committees, 180 ; County organizations, 181 ; District Committees, 181 ; outfit, 181 ; training centres, 182 ; forestry timber supply and forage, 183 ; seasonal labour, 183 ; mobility of Land Army, 183 ; wages, 184–185 ; billeting, 185 ; leisure time, 185 ; women's special aptitudes, 188 ; as shepherds, 189 ; examples of courage, 190 ; demobilization date, 191 ; gratitude of the nation, 193
Wool, price of, 22
Worlidge (1669), drilling, sowing and manuring, 43, 52

YARRANTON, Andrew (1653), 40.
Yearly tenants, 7
Young, Arthur, 40, 48